1001 Questions Answered:
GROWING FOOD UNDER GLASS

In the Same Series
Growing Vegetables
Growing Fruit

By the Same Authors
Plant Propagation in Pictures
Garden Construction in Pictures

1001 QUESTIONS ANSWERED

GROWING FOOD UNDER GLASS

ADRIENNE & PETER OLDALE

David & Charles
Newton Abbot London North Pomfret (Vt) Vancouver

British Library Cataloguing in Publication Data

Oldale, Adrienne
  Growing food under glass. – (1001 questions answered).
  1. Greenhouse plants   2. Vegetable gardening
  3. Fruit-culture
  I. Title II. Oldale, Peter   III. Series
  635'.04'44   SB352

  ISBN 0–7153–7334–X

Library of Congress Catalog Card Number 77–85012

Set in 9 on 10pt Helvetica by
Trade Linotype Limited Birmingham
and printed in Great Britain by
Biddles Limited Guildford
for David & Charles (Publishers) Limited
Brunel House Newton Abbot Devon

Published in the United States of America
by David & Charles Inc
North Pomfret Vermont 05053 USA

Published in Canada
by Douglas David & Charles Limited
1875 Welch Street North Vancouver BC

Contents

Table of Imperial and Metric Measures

Length

1in		=	2.5cm
3in		=	7.6cm
6in		=	15.2cm
9in		=	22.8cm
12in	= 1ft	=	30.5cm
3ft	= 1yd	=	0.9m
2yd		=	1.8m

Weight

1oz	=	28.4g
1lb	=	450g
1cwt	=	51kg

Capacity

1pt		=	570ml
2pt	= 1 quart	=	1.14l
8pt	= 1 gal	=	4.5l

Area

1sq ft	=	930sq cm
1sq yd	=	8400sq cm

How to Use this Book

Almost every gardener growing food eventually wonders if glass could help produce good crops. Cold frames, heated frames, simple cloches or full-sized greenhouses can indeed all be used to give us heavier, better quality produce over a longer season.

This book tells you all you need to know when setting out to grow food under glass, starting perhaps with the simplest and cheapest of equipment, or even in the home, on a bright window sill.

As with our other books in this *1001 Questions Answered* series, you can read it straight through, the questions following each other in a simple, conversational manner. If you wish, though, you can also treat it as a reference book, for special information needed at any time.

The first part consists of a series of questions on different, important topics, such as starting out, choosing a greenhouse site, the different types and materials available, preparing the site and erecting the structure. Interior fittings come next, with long sections on greenhouse heating and lighting, equipment for ventilation and watering, maintenance and soil preparation.

It is important to understand the basic, simple techniques used in glass work generally, so there are a whole series of questions on seed sowing, border culture, growing in rings or on straw bales, also on greenhouse hygiene and control of pests and diseases.

The second part of the book is in alphabetical order of the crop names, from Apricots to Tomatoes. Here you will find, in logical order, clear information about the needs of each crop, in soil, temperature, light, fertilizers, pruning, diseases, treatment and harvesting.

By reading the first part, you should get a pretty accurate picture of glasshouse work generally (including the inexpensive but efficient cloches and frames). For detailed facts about specific plants, look these up in the alphabetic section.

One problem always faces a gardening writer — the very wide range of climate, site, equipment and structure that might be used for growing a particular crop. Your own garden may be in the soft-aired, long summers of the South West, or the hard, tough climate of the North East. Your greenhouse may be small or large, powerfully heated or cold, windswept or sheltered. When using our answers then, bear in mind the problem of covering all these possibilities, and use care if your situation is in any way extreme — hot or cold, wet or dry and so on.

Gardening is half a science, half an art. This book can, we believe, pass on some of the knowledge we have acquired through years of gardening, getting it right or — sometimes — getting it wrong! We hope that it will start you off, or help you further along the way, in the pleasant task of producing crops of better quality, earlier (and later!) in the season and in greater amounts than is possible out-of-doors.

These days, with food prices rising ever faster, and truly garden-fresh produce more difficult to find, there is more reason than ever to get yourself some glass and start producing food for yourself and your family.

Part 1
Technique and Preparation

Why Bother with Glass?

1 *Why do so many gardeners use glass in one way or another?*

To get earlier, higher quality crops of greater weight. Also to grow food that could otherwise not be produced in our climate. The smallest garden benefits from even a single row of cloches.

2 *Are cloches the simple two sheets of glass propped up over crops?*

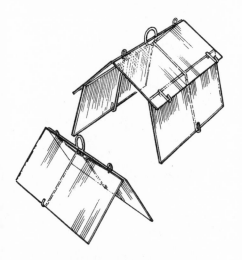

This indeed is the simplest 'tent' type. You can get bigger sorts, though, with removable side panes supported on wire frames. Some are even tall enough to accommodate tomatoes.

3 *What plants benefit from using cloches?*

Most early crops and those that are still developing when cold weather sets in during autumn. The air under well arranged cloches is distinctly warmer than outside.

4 *Are garden frames always better than cloches?*

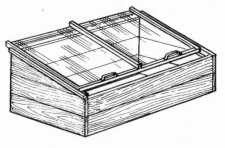

Not necessarily. They have different purposes. Cloches are usually placed over crops seeded in rows outdoors. They can be easily removed as the plants develop, or weather improves, and used somewhere else. Cold frames, on the other hand, are usually (but not always) fixed. Their purpose is either for propagation of seeds and cuttings, forcing or producing low growing plants such as lettuce, under warm and controlled conditions.

5 *Presumably heated frames grow a wider range of crops than cool ones?*

Yes. Being small in volume, frames cost little in fuel and are particularly good for rampant growing crops like melons and cucumbers which, though desirable, may take up a lot of room in an expensively heated greenhouse.

6 *How useful is a small amateur greenhouse for actual food growing?*

Greenhouse crops are prolific and produce far more food than the same area of open land or even frames. You can also grow tall crops such as the tomato, not to mention pot plants and flowers for the home at most times of the year.

7 *Does greenhouse work need a lot of skill?*

Not at first. You can start with easy crops and get useful results in a few months. Of course, you will learn as you go along and can expect steady improvement and an increasing value of crops.

8 *In strictest cash terms, can a small*

greenhouse show a profit?

Yes, though of course it does depend upon what you grow and the skill with which you manage the work. Given good plant hygiene, regular attention to ventilation and watering and careful control of the heat level, 90 per cent of home gardeners should make money on their greenhouse.

9 *Does this include the original cost of the greenhouse and its equipment?*

Yes, spread over some years. Modern, good quality greenhouses will last almost indefinitely with only a modest amount of maintenance. They are a good investment.

10 *Surely I shall get produce just when there is a glut on the market?*

Sometimes, but as you gain in skill you will be able to plan your crops to suit your needs and for times when they are scarce.

11 *What are the main foods I can expect to get from a greenhouse?*

Tomatoes, cucumbers, lettuce and other salads are the basic crops, but in addition you can grow all your own vegetable plants for outdoors, so getting early crops economically.

12 *I cannot afford much time every day in the garden. Do greenhouses call for very frequent attention?*

At the height of the growing season they need ventilation and perhaps watering daily. Fortunately, though, quite simple devices will help you a lot with these chores, opening vents automatically and providing a regular water flow. In any case, the daily time taken is only minutes.

13 *Can you sum up the main purposes served by cloches, frames and greenhouses?*

Cloches are a valuable help to outdoor gardening. Most crops grown in rows will gain two or three weeks if housed in cloches in their early life. You can seed earlier with better germination. They are portable, cheap and, apart from glass breakage, last indefinitely. Unheated frames give useful protection to early sowings of seeds in boxes and can be used like cloches to produce early crops of low growing plants. In conjunction with a greenhouse or heated frame they can also be used to 'harden off' plants before moving them outside.

Heated frames serve almost like greenhouses for low growing crops and will produce heavy crops for their size and cost.

Greenhouses can be organized and heated to provide food crops all the year round, as well as germinating seeds for outdoor use. In them you can grow tall plants such as tomatoes, or even trees such as apricots, peaches and, of course, grapes.

Growing Food in the Home

14 *Is it possible to grow useful food plants inside a house or flat with no outside greenhouse or frame?*

Plants will grow wherever they have soil, warmth, water and light, so in principle there is nothing against growing plants inside a house. The limitation is usually light because houses are darker inside than they appear to our eyes.

15 *Surely some plants grow in the dark and many are forced in dark places?*

Only fungi can live in total darkness. Mushrooms can certainly be grown. Forcing plants is a different procedure. You then take a plant which has already developed adequate food reserves in its roots and stems and put it in a warm, dark place to encourage it to push out leaves. Such leaves are always very pale or even totally white. They cannot form green chlorophyll without light. The plant draws all its growth from its existing food stocks, so forced roots are nearly always useless afterwards.

16 *Given adequate light, what is the main problem when growing food indoors?*

Watering. Houses are usually warm enough for the growth to go on but the plants in this state do need keeping moist. In a greenhouse or frame the surplus water drains away into the soil. This will not happen in your living room! You have to make provision for trapping surplus water.

17 *How can this be done?*

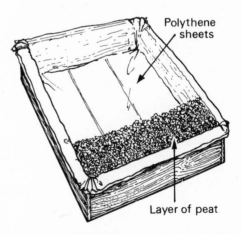
Polythene sheets

Layer of peat

There are several ways, all involving providing a waterproof tray on which the plants are stood. The simplest method is to arrange two or three layers of uncut polythene sheet (quite cheaply bought from builders' merchants) over a rectangle of wood 6in deep. Fold the corners carefully so that water draining from the plants cannot escape.

18 *Does it help to make such trays, then fill them with peat moss?*

This is excellent if you are growing plants in pots. The peat can be moistened and acts as a reserve water supply, as well as maintaining a humid atmosphere near the plants.

19 *Since all green plants require light, presumably the best place for them is a south-facing windowsill?*

Not always. You have to consider the likely room temperature all through day and night. Consider a room which is little used at night with a south-facing window. Heat may build up during the day to quite a considerable degree but be followed by an extremely cool night. This is not good for most plants. An even temperature is much more important than a high maximum.

20 *Do plants grow best in living rooms then?*

They would probably do better because the night temperature is likely to remain higher, though there may be more draughts as people move about. Centrally heated rooms are perhaps best of all if you can control the heaters to give a fairly even temperature throughout the 24 hours.

21 *Most of my brightest rooms face north. Does this make plant growing difficult?*

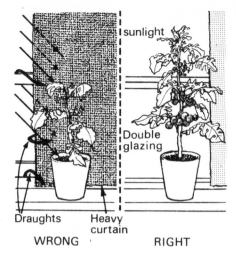

Draughts   Heavy
           curtain
    WRONG   RIGHT

Yes, though not absolutely impossible. It depends how cold the area next to the window becomes at night. Often a cold draught develops around windows after the sun goes down. Any plants standing in this will be severely affected. Drawing the curtains can help a lot and, of course, double glazing almost entirely prevents it.

22 *If I grow plants on window sills, is it best to keep the window itself open or shut during the day?*

If the temperatures are high enough for the plant, always allow it plenty of ventilation. This doesn't mean, of course, that you want an icy cold draught blowing in from outside into a warm room. Broadly speaking, plants like the type of conditions which we like ourselves. Not too hot, not too cold and without cold draughts.

23 *We have gas central heating. Will this affect plants we grow indoors?*

No, provided your equipment is properly vented. Gas fumes from ovens and so on do affect plants though, and you may have difficulties in a kitchen, or in other rooms heated by open flame gas heaters.

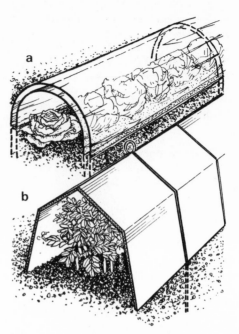

24 *Is it really worthwhile to attempt to grow food plants inside the home?*

They are an agreeable novelty and some sorts such as miniature tomatoes can give moderate crops. However, you are obviously not likely to get as successful results as with even the simplest of greenhouses. Conditions inside a home are usually fairly dark, irregular in temperature and either too draughty or, sometimes, too humid. A greenhouse after all is controlled for the benefit of the plants; a house for the benefit of humans! The needs of these are not always the same. Do not expect too big crops therefore, but enjoy the novelty of it all.

Starting Out — Cloches and Frames

25 *Cloches can be made of glass or various kinds of plastic. Is there anything to choose between these?*

Glass still tends to be cheapest. The panes only require simple wire supports (you can make these yourself). Glass is also the best conserver of the sun's heat. Plastics differ in price quite considerably. Ordinary polythene sheet does not have the same heat-conserving effect as glass, so it is less effective in cold weather. Always use it double, the skins separated by 1in. Rigid plastic cloches, however, are often of a horticultural type that does have heat-conserving qualities. They are very light and can be firmly joined in long lengths, so avoiding the draughty joints which are almost unavoidable with small glass panes. Plastics are very tough, but in a windy area may

blow away unless pegged down.

26 *How are cloches best used?*

Their purpose is to raise the temperature of the soil and air beneath them. If possible, put a row of cloches in place a week or two before sowing seeds. This warms the soil a little and may keep it drier in what may be a wet spring. Replace the cloches quickly after sowing. Make sure the ends of the 'tunnels' are blocked with a sheet of glass or wood (failures with cloches are often due to wind rushing through the open ends).

27 *How can I water crops under cloches?*

In most parts, the spring soil is damp enough for seedlings to grow quite tall before watering is needed. In any case, the gaps between the cloches allow a certain amount of rainwater to gain access. If you do water, remove the whole row, sprinkle and then replace. Do not overdo watering under cloches.

28 *Is there any artificial way of warming crops under cloches?*

Not as a rule, though a few gardeners have tried a dug-in soil warming cable (see pages 16, 38–9) run under the row before sowing.

29 *Can tall crops like tomatoes be grown under cloches?*

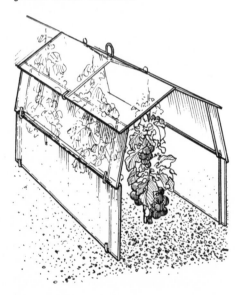

Yes. Choose tomato varieties that are not too vigorous (your nurseryman will advise on suitable varieties for your area) and buy tall glass 'barn type' cloches with removable side panes. With big cloches, adequate ventilation becomes more important.

30 *What plants can be forced under cloches?*

This depends on your situation. In cold windy areas, forcing really calls for a secure, warm structure such as a frame or greenhouse. In mild areas you could try your luck with globe beet sown in midwinter, carrots, chives, onions, peas, potatoes, radishes, and herbs such as mint and tarragon. (You will find more details under these names in the second part of the book.)

31 *Commercially made garden frames seem expensive. Is it possible to make your own satisfactorily?*

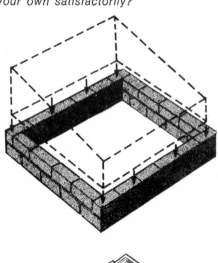

Yes, any normal material will serve with concrete, bricks or wood for the walls.

14

Over these simply fix a framed glass sheet tilted at an angle to let the rain pass off freely. Make them 18in high above the soil at the rear, sloping to about 12in in front.

32 *I find the greatest difficulty in making up the glass frames. Can I use polythene sheet instead, which is much cheaper and easier to fix?*

This is possible, though polythene does not have much 'greenhouse effect' in trapping sunlight. Use it double, on lightweight wooden frames, and it will help retain the natural heat of the frame and of course protect the plants within from cool winds. Such frames are light and cheap. You can make a large size frame for only a pound or two, probably less than a tenth of a comparable area of glass or rigid plastic, and it is much easier to handle. Of course, it will not last so long.

33 *How long a life can I expect of a polythene frame-light?*

The plastic itself should be replaced every two years, but if you treat the wood frame with proper preservative (not creosote) this should last almost indefinitely. Make sure, however, that the frames are held well down, especially in a windy area.

34 *There are some rigid transparent sheets of plastic of various makes. Can these be used for satisfactory frames?*

Yes, especially if the plastic is of a kind prepared for horticultural work. These materials can often be nailed or screwed to simple wooden frames and, being rigid, are stronger and much longer lasting than polythene. They do, however, cost much more.

35 *If I buy a ready-made frame, are there any special points to watch for?*

Be sure that the framing of the glass is strong and well jointed. This is where trouble arises because the frame top must be frequently lifted or propped open. This puts it under twisting stress. The sides of the frame itself should, of course, be resistant to rot and reasonably strong. Some commercial frames are really not deep enough but this can often be corrected by erecting them on a rectangle of closely set cemented house bricks.

36 *Which direction should frames face —towards the midday sun?*

Yes, or rather westwards of this. Certainly for food growing they need to be in a light position.

37 *What winter treatment do frames require?*

Frames harbour insect pests and diseases. It is vital to clean them well preferably using formalin or similar sterilising agent to get rid of as many as possible of such future hazards.

38 *I have a cold frame. What advantage would I get from providing heating?*

A heated frame can be in use throughout the year. Cold frames must remain unoccupied until the spring sun starts to warm them and in winter can only partly shelter hardy plants. With heat you can often start seedlings into growth weeks or even months early, and keep a steady flow of young crops warm in winter. Forcing plants too calls for heat.

39 *What is the most easily controlled way of heating frames?*

Electric soil warming cables. These are buried 9in deep in the soil and the comparatively low current will give a steady and controlled heat. They are, though, fairly expensive to buy. Other systems include hanging similar electric wires on special supports round the sides of the frame to heat the air. This is an advantage in frosty periods. You can also get very small oil heaters which will keep out the frost, but we have not tried these ourselves. A hotbed was the old method, and costs nothing if you have a supply of farm or stable manure.

40 *What exactly is a hotbed and how does it work?*

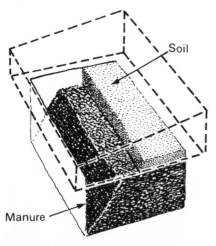

Soil

Manure

Hotbeds are layers of rather fresh manure buried within the frame. When manure rots, it heats up, warming the soil and air above. To make one, dig a 2ft deep hole almost the size of the frame and nearly fill this with fresh or partly rotted manure. Cover this with several inches of soil. The bed generates heat for anything up to eight weeks and used to be a common method for starting off such things as cucumbers.

41 *Can you really get much heat from manure like this?*

Ample, though it is a little difficult to control at first. You may even have to open the bed sometimes (by digging a vent hole down to the manure) to release surplus energy.

42 *What is the commonest mistake made in growing plants in frames?*

Giving too little ventilation. Plants can be killed just as effectively by depriving them of air as they can be by frost. It is especially important in warm spring days after cool nights.

43 *Are pests and diseases a problem in frame growing?*

Wherever we grow crops there are always risks, and these are greater in warm moist conditions such as we try to develop in the frames. However, the control methods described later on are quite easy to apply.

Moving On — To a Greenhouse

44 *Is a greenhouse most useful in cold, moderate or warm parts of the country?*

A greenhouse is of some use everywhere but probably gives most effective service in moderate parts where small amounts of fuel can extend the normal growing season well beyond spring and summer. The costs are relatively low in relation to the advantage, and all through winter you can have the benefit of a heated greenhouse. In cold areas you need more fuel and usually the available light is much less.

45 *Does low light really matter? Surely*

it is warmth that plants mainly need?

No. Light is the main essential. Without it, plants cannot convert soil chemicals into food. Indeed, rapid growth induced by greenhouse warmth will call for higher light levels than outdoors.

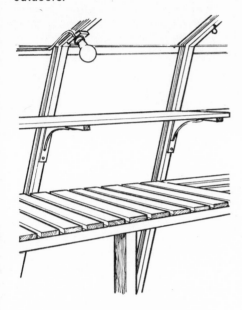

46 *Presumably heating costs are lowest in warm areas?*

Naturally, although in the far South-West, it is so warm and sunny that you may not really need a greenhouse at all! If you do have one, your problem may be keeping the heat down and maintaining adequate ventilation. It is often easier to warm up a greenhouse than to cool it!

47 *Is it an advantage to live near the coast?*

Yes, on the whole. The great mass of the sea moderates all extreme temperatures as well as reflecting more light. The main risk is exposure to much stronger winds than inland, which can sometimes damage the glass. The flow of cooling air can also raise heating costs.

48 *I live near a big city. Will the pollution in the air affect greenhouse plants?*

This is only serious in rather extreme cases. You will probably get more trouble from dirt obscuring the glass. Smoke, fog, and the shade of buildings too can lower light levels. Choose as open a position as possible, and be prepared to wash down the glass at least once or twice a year.

49 *We live in a rather hilly area inland. Is this good country for a greenhouse?*

If you are on the south or west-facing slope of a hill and not too near the bottom you will gain maximum benefit from the sunshine. Northern and eastern slopes are not so good, but height usually improves the availability of light. The main problems in hills are that they often attract a high rainfall and so there may be frequent cloudy spells. Valley bottoms may be frost traps. Exposed slopes may be windy.

50 *From what you say, every area of the country has some disadvantage!*

This is true, but few things in this life are perfect! If you know the particular problems in your sort of country you can take steps to correct them or adjust your growing programme to suit.

51 *Can you give general ideas of the way to deal with these various difficulties, starting with the coast?*

17

Wind is the usual trouble, so provide shelter belts of trees or fencing to deflect the worst of the gales. Check your greenhouse structure thoroughly and regularly (aluminium often corrodes near sea water). Site doors away from the usual wind. See that window ventilation controls are free and easy to operate.

52 What about cold, flat areas inland?

Wind will still be troublesome, so once again, provide windbreak shelter and a really efficient heating system. Good surface drainage will be needed too.

53 Ours is a cloudy area with moderate hills. Presumably we should keep the greenhouse well away from shade?

Yes. This is important. Indeed, for some purposes, artificial lighting for part of the season may be useful, but this does call for skill in effective use. Aluminium is good here. It lets in more light than wood.

54 Our district is actually quite warm in all but the depths of winter. What will our main problems be?

Keeping cool! Choose a wide open site. You will need extra large ventilators, even fan extractors. If a little broken shade, such as from a large tree, is available this may be useful.

55 I am moving soon to a new house. How can I find out the amount of sunshine and cloud to be expected there?

Meteorological records often are kept in public libraries. Local papers help too, or the nearest weather forecast office. However, let us repeat that

there are very few places where a greenhouse is not useful, provided the limitations of its situation are realised and allowed for.

56 Should I have a soil analysis done before deciding to buy a greenhouse?

Soil analysis is always useful because it tells you what plant foods may be in short supply and the amount of lime needed. However, the amount of soil in a greenhouse is so small that almost any sort can be made fertile reasonably easily (see pages 47–9). At the same time, ask for a check on the presence of the potato root eelworm. This pest can savagely attack tomatoes.

57 Must I have planning permission to erect a greenhouse?

Usually not, but this depends upon various local regulations, on the greenhouse size and its relation to the size and position of the house. It is far better to make enquiries at your local authority than to go ahead and then have to alter things later. Manufacturers of all greenhouses will happily supply you free with suitable plans for applications. Apart from these, you may have to supply a 'block plan' which is simply a drawing of your garden showing the position of the greenhouse in relation to your house.

58 What other information will usually be needed?

The material and general design of the greenhouse will be given by the manufacturers. You may have to say what kind of foundations and perhaps drains you intend to install.

59 I want to build my own greenhouse,

not buy one ready-made. Will the council accept my simple drawings?

All they want are:
1 The exact size of the structure.
2 The shape from front, side and top.
3 An idea of its appearance, materials, etc.

If you can draw a simple, scale plan, perhaps on squared paper, this will often do perfectly well. The authority will always ask for any information you may have left out.

60 *Can I connect greenhouse drains to our house drainage system?*

Never—at least, not without skilled help and the permission of your local council.

61 *I live in a rented property. Will I have to ask my landlord's permission to put up a greenhouse?*

This depends upon the terms of your lease, but as a general rule it is far better to consult the landlord and your solicitor first. The laws of ownership of buildings on land are complicated and you might end up building a greenhouse which at once becomes your landlord's property.

62 *Do I have to ask my neighbours before erecting a greenhouse?*

It is always as well, when applying for planning permission, to have the agreement of neighbours though this is not a legal requirement as a rule.

63 *What are the main shapes of greenhouse to choose from?*

Span-roofed, lean-to or circular. Of course, the actual proportions can vary widely. A lean-to is erected against a wall and usually faces south. A span-

roof type will often have its ridge running north–south. Circular ones mainly vary in the position of the door, usually hung away from the prevailing wind.

64 *Some houses have glass right down to the ground and others have solid side walls with glass above. Why is this?*

Side wall greenhouses are best used for growing plants in pots, tubs, or boxes on benches. Walls can be made thicker and more heat-retaining than glass. They are easier to warm since glass-to-ground greenhouses are mainly for plants requiring maximum light which are usually planted in the soil. Seedlings or pot plants need all the heat they can get and can dispense with some light at ground level, but food crops in general need all the light possible.

65 *What are the advantages of lean-to greenhouses?*

The building against which they are built insulates them on at least one side and makes them substantially easier to heat. They cost considerably less, size for size, than any other type. The main disadvantage is that they may be shaded by the house itself, for part of the day at least. This is a serious problem. A lean-to must face the sun or it will be very little use for food growing.

66 *Span-roof types seem to be most popular. What are their main advantages?*

They are simple enough to make, especially in mass production, so their cost can be kept down. Properly sited, they trap most of the available light and heat, and their plan makes it easy

19

to put up shelves, arrange boxes and pots, etc.

67 *Fixing things like that in circular greenhouses might well be a problem. Is there any real advantage in this shape?*

Yes. Round houses probably have the highest volume of usable area in relation to their overall size. They admit light freely from all sides and are very comfortable to work in, because you stand in one place, merely turning round to reach the different parts of bench, water supply, etc. Their main disadvantages are that they cost more and in general are on the small side. You do need a fair amount of space for cucumbers or tomatoes which are, after all, our main greenhouse crops.

68 *What is a Dutch light house?*

Usually a span-roofed house made from frames bolted together around large sheets of glass. The panes are roughly 4ft by 2ft, so four joined in span shape make a low house that can be fairly easily altered in length or moved from place to place. They are much used commercially but less by amateurs.

69 *What are their main benefits and defects?*

Dutch lights cost less than the same area of conventional glass. They admit light well and are versatile. You can take the houses apart and use the panels as frame lights. Defects are the cost of the glass if broken, the low height, difficulties with ventilation and a rather crude appearance.

70 *Are there any special points to look for in the design of the greenhouse?*

Check ventilators. There should be facility for opening at the roof and low down, for air exit and entry, and these should be duplicated on opposite sides to allow for the wind direction. Doorways must be wide enough for your wheelbarrow! Much of greenhouse work involves carting bulky materials, compost, soil cleared plants, etc. Easy access makes for comfort.

71 *Some of the large or medium-sized houses have division walls separating them into two parts. Are these worth the cost?*

Yes. They enable you to heat up a small area for special plants such as cucumbers, without the waste of overheating the rest.

72 *Can you summarise the advantages of lean-to, span, Dutch light, and circular houses?*

LEAN-TO
Cheap, strong, easy to heat and a pleasant 'home extension'.
SPAN
Businesslike, efficient, strong and a wide range available at moderate prices.
DUTCH LIGHT
Versatile, easily erected and extended, moderate cost.
CIRCULAR
Very efficient for their size and often attractive structures in their own right, so can be used decoratively on lawns.

Greenhouse Materials

73 *Is there one ideal material for a greenhouse?*

No. All have some advantages, and some defects. It is a matter worth looking at carefully before you buy. Many different materials have been used, hardwoods, softwoods, aluminium and its alloys, steel, cast iron, plus, of course, brick, stone and concrete for lower walls.

74 *Some of the materials are surely old-fashioned now?*

Cast iron is obsolete, but there are still fine old houses standing made with beautiful framings. Hardwoods too are little used for amateur houses, due to their increasing cost, but again, you might take over an old garden with a house in this material.

75 *Aluminium or softwoods seem the commonest modern structures. Are there different types of these materials?*

Aluminium is often an alloy, since pure aluminium is relatively soft. Wooden houses are, broadly speaking, of three sorts: painted softwood, pressure treated softwoods or cedarwood.

76 *What should I look for in the metal kinds?*

Aluminium is expensive still, so makers working down to a price may use over-light sections. Some you can easily bend between your fingers. When comparing prices, note the sizes and apparent strength of the bars used, and their fastenings.

77 *Is it true that aluminium houses last only a few years at the seaside?*

There is some truth in this, if the coast is subject to strong onshore winds. Salty, moist air attacks all metals, and aluminium is more susceptible than some. Painting protects the metal for a time, but one of the prime

advantages of aluminium generally is that it needs no maintenance. In places where corrosion is likely, rot-proof wood might be a better choice.

78 *The glass in metal houses appears to be held in only by little bent wires. Is this method strong enough?*

With few exceptions, all the commercially used methods give good results. If your home is exceptionally exposed to strong winds, it might be worth checking with the makers whether extra clips would be helpful.

79 *From the plants' point of view, has metal any special advantages?*

Yes. It harbours few pests and diseases, and in any case is easy to clean. Of lesser importance is that the metal frames are usually thinner than wood and let in more light.

80 *What advantages do painted softwood houses have?*

Low price, though the difference may not be marked. Also, as with all wooden houses, they are easier than metal to alter, add to or repair. Shelves and staging can be fastened to the glazing bars, as also can fitments for polythene lining, mountings for lights and other equipment.

81 *Can these things not be fixed to metal?*

Yes, but most of us have tools and skills mainly relating to wood. For metal attachments, you need drills, screws and nuts, pop-rivet guns, metal saws, etc.

82 *What main disadvantage does painted softwood have?*

The need for painting — usually every year — and the chance of rot if this is not thoroughly done. Sometimes the wood on cheap models is badly seasoned, and splits and cracks appear or joints part. Pressure-treated softwood is better. Painting can be less frequent and usually the quality of timber is higher.

83 *Cedarwood is often advertised as 'rot-proof'. Is this claim true?*

Yes, broadly speaking. Rot in red cedar is rare but cedar is 50 per cent weaker than most timbers so needs extra thickness. It is a point to watch in the cheaper models.

84 *Is cedar easy to work with, for repairs, etc?*

Yes. It is extremely soft. This very quality, though, makes it necessary to use fatter screws, to hold firmly in the wood.

85 *In general, is it better to have large glass panes, or small ones?*

Large for light, small for strength. If you live in an exposed gale-ridden area do not buy houses with the biggest panes. You need the strength of closer spaced timber.

86 *Does the glass itself vary in quality?*

Glass differs in weight and in its clarity. It is measured in ounces per square foot (grams per square metre), 24oz and 32oz being usual. Horticultural glass is not completely clear, but serves the plants just as well as clear. Heavier glass is not necessarily best. The sheer weight imposes a load on the structure. Large panes should be of heavy glass, but

small panes can be much thinner.

87 *Can you sum up the pros and cons of each main material?*

Painted Softwood
Cheap. Serviceable if painted regularly, weak if neglected. Joints may be poor. Good for fixings.

Pressure-heated Softwood
Moderate price. Needs retreatment every two or three years. Good for fixings, withstands sea air.

Cedarwood
Moderate to expensive. Rot-proof, only needs treatment to preserve colour. Thin sections are weak. Heavy sections slightly reduce light. Fixings need oversize screws. Best for seaside.

Aluminium
Moderate to expensive. Normally needs no maintenance, gives good light to plants. Cheap models may have thin metal sections. Many have large glass panes and may be weak in winds. Often corrodes near sea water. Awkward for fixings.

88 *I have seen greenhouses made with plastic instead of glass. Presumably the advantages and defects are similar to those when used for frames?*

Yes, with more emphasis still on the the light weight of polythene covered structures. Even moderate winds can do severe damage. The stiff wire or plastic net reinforced sheeting is better, whilst rigid plastic sheet, usually corrugated, can make quite a serviceable, long lasting greenhouse. Choose only material recommended for horticultural use. Others may have different heat-retaining capacities.

22

Choosing the Site—Shelter and Water Supplies

89 *What are the main points to watch in siting a new greenhouse?*

1, Good light; 2, shelter from cold winds; 3, ample water supplies; 4, easy access from the house, and 5, reasonable drainage, in that order.

90 *To get most light I suppose all that is needed is to put the greenhouse well away from anything tall such as a house, trees, etc?*

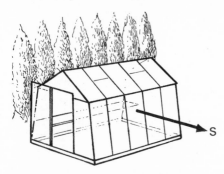

Not necessarily. First check the direction and height of the sun at midday (bear in mind that it will be lower in winter than in summer). Sunshine comes from one side only, so if need be the other side might well be placed near to the house or to a shelter belt of tall trees.

91 *In my garden there is simply no place where the greenhouse can be placed to get sun all day. Which is more important, morning or afternoon sun?*

Afternoon. This is brighter and usually warmer, so aim for most light from the west.

92 *Does it matter which way a span-roof greenhouse runs, north–south or east–west?*

In an open situation, line it up north–south. Then plants on both sides will get equal amounts of sun. An east–west arrangement will result in plants at one side being partly shaded by plants growing up the other, sunward side.

93 *I have certainly seen greenhouses arranged east–west. Are these all incorrect?*

Not necessarily. There may be shadowing obstructions on one side, or the gardener may be growing a mixture of tall, light-loving plants such as tomatoes and house plants, or flowers in pots which do not require so much sun. These can be grown on the shadier wall.

94 *On which wall should a lean-to greenhouse be built?*

Ideally, on one facing the noon or afternoon sun. If the only wall available is on the shady side of the house it would be far better to build instead a smaller, span-roof greenhouse out in the light.

95 *At which end of a span-roof house should I put the door?*

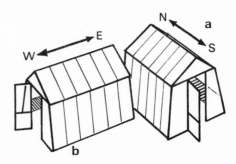

If the house runs north–south, on the sunward end. If it runs east–west on the west end (except perhaps in coastal areas where strong westerly winds are common).

96 *Your second main requirement was shelter from cold winds. How can this best be provided?*

By shelter belts of modest sized trees which break the full force of cold winds; by openwork fencing on the same side or by placing the greenhouse to the sunnier side of the house which can then act as a windbreak.

97 *Can't I get good wind shelter by placing a greenhouse between my house and next door?*

Not usually, even if the light is adequate. Wind often funnels through gaps between houses and creates immense heating problems.

98 *How high should shelter fencing be erected?*

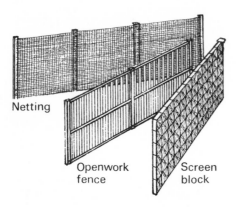

Netting

Openwork fence   Screen block

Not less than 6ft. Even fairly cheap materials are suitable, such as closely woven netting, whether of jute or

plastic, erected on strong wooden posts. For a stronger job, use openwork fencing such as fairly close mesh trellis, well braced against the prevailing wind.

99 *Why not use solid fencing such as overlapped timber? Surely this would be stronger and more effective?*

In practice, a solid fence tends to cause winds to eddy over its top and create blustery, draughty conditions just beside the greenhouse itself. More open structures such as partial overlap or openweave fencing allows some of the wind to pass through but at a restricted speed and without so much eddying.

100 *Presumably then, concrete or brick walls are not desirable?*

Only those kinds which are built in an openwork pattern, or of concrete blocks commonly known as screen blocks, with holes through them.

101 *What sort of trees can be used for a shelter belt?*

Any that grow reasonably thickly near their bases. Poplars are rapid-growing but do have rather searching roots. They should be kept away from domestic buildings as a rule. The various thujas and cupressus type trees grow more slowly and are not everywhere entirely hardy, but they do form a good screen. Hedges of beech, privet or thorn are all good but, of course, take some years to reach the necessary height.

102 *How near should greenhouses be placed to a shelter belt of trees?*

Not nearer than about 12ft. Nearer, there will be tree roots spreading out

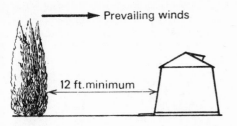

Prevailing winds

12 ft. minimum

into the greenhouse borders. These might even damage the foundations.

103 *Your third main requirement was a good water supply. Surely it is enough to be able to fetch water in cans from a tap in the house or garage?*

It is certainly possible, but few things are as inconvenient in greenhouse work as a shortage of water. If you have to fetch water from any distance it soon becomes a tiring chore. In the height of summer you might need thirty or forty cans a day!

104 *What about a long hose reaching right from tap to greenhouse?*

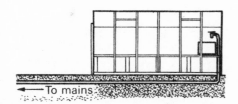

To mains

This is better though flexible piping does tend to wear, kink or puncture. A good quality, non-kinkable pipe will prove well worth its extra expense. The best type of water supply is an underground, permanent pipe with a tap and a large storage tank in the greenhouse itself.

105 *It would be expensive to get a plumber to install a pipe like that. Can the job be done properly by an amateur?*

Certainly, and the job need be no worse done either, with modern materials and methods. The hardest parts are the preparation of the trench, refilling it when the pipe has been laid, and cutting any necessary holes through to the house or greenhouse structure.

106 *Will I need planning permission?*

Not usually, but you certainly should discuss the idea first with your local water authority. Their engineers are always most helpful if they are consulted early.

107 *What sort of questions will be asked?*

Mainly the exact position of the greenhouse in relation to the house, the length of pipe, and place you want to connect it, etc.

108 *What materials are best?*

Buy alkathene black plastic piping. This will not burst if frozen, as it remains slightly flexible. The joint systems used are very simple. You will only need a couple of large adjustable spanners.

109 *How do I make the final connection to the water main?*

Many water boards will not allow you to connect such a system direct to their mains unless most of the work is done by a professional plumber. This you will have to discover before starting. What they will often allow is a tap connection.

110 *Does this mean I can fit the pipe to an already existing outside tap?*

Yes, as a rule. Don't forget to lag the pipe against frost where it is exposed, between the tap and the trench.

111 *Would such an arrangement be a hose-pipe? Many restrictions are often placed on the use of hoses during dry summers.*

This depends upon the local authority concerned, but most are anxious to restrict the use of hose-pipes for non-essential work such as car cleaning or lawn spraying rather than for food growing.

112 *How big a pipe is needed for a greenhouse?*

This depends upon the pressure of water in your own system and also what sort of equipment you are going to have. Most amateurs will have an ample supply using only a $\frac{1}{2}$in diameter plastic pipe. A pipe more than 30ft long would be better with a $\frac{3}{4}$in bore, because of friction.

113 *I am thinking of using mist propagation units and automatic irrigation. Will this increase the required diameter of the pipe?*

It will certainly then be better to fit a 1in pipe. If pressure is fairly low in your district, use big bores and keep all pipe runs as short as possible.

114 *Our town water is treated with chemicals. Are these likely to affect plants' growth?*

No. Chemicals employed for purification and fluoridation have no significant affect on amateur grown plants.

115 *The fourth of your essentials was good access. Do you mean that the greenhouse must be near the house?*

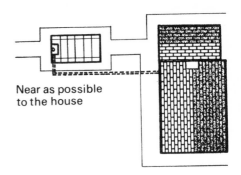

Near as possible to the house

Yes. This may seem a rather obvious point but it is worth considering carefully. The success of greenhouse work depends upon regular attention to comparatively small items such as vent closing and adjustment, watering, etc. If the greenhouse is far away you may put off doing some of these vital jobs, with sad results for the plants. A good path to and fro is also desirable.

116 *Surely, by bringing it near to the house I may shade the glass and lose some sunlight?*

This is true, but all gardening is a compromise. You have to balance the risk of neglecting plants in a distant greenhouse against loss of light if it is placed nearer.

117 *Your last essential was good ground drainage. Why is this so vital?*

Good drainage is more important under a greenhouse than under a lawn or flowerbed. Stagnant, wet conditions inside can rapidly lead to attacks of mould or other diseases. In a warm atmosphere such attacks can be very severe.

118 *Surely this is only important if the plants are actually grown in the borders. I intend to grow my plants on straw bales or in boxes.*

Even then you would find it very uncomfortable to have a soggy earth floor, which will also be cold and increase your heating costs.

119 *Can you sum up all these points in deciding where to erect a greenhouse?*

Get as much light as possible, shelter from cold and good drainage. Make sure you have good water supplies. Build as near to the back door as is consistent with all these needs.

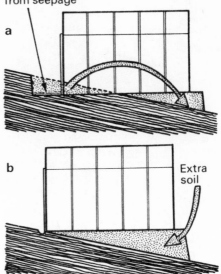

Possible accumulation from seepage

a

b

Extra soil

Site Preparation, Drainage, Foundations and Erection

120 *What is the first step in preparing the site for a greenhouse?*

First find out whether you need drainage. If your garden slopes for example, you may need none, though this can depend on the way the site is arranged.

121 *How can the site plan affect drainage?*

To get a level site on a slope, you usually dig out at the back, up the slope, and use the dug soil to raise the front level, down the slope. You may then get water accumulating at the back, where it soaks down the resulting steep bank.

122 *What method of levelling can avoid this?*

Get extra soil from somewhere, and raise the front level without digging

out at the rear. Here is a side view of both methods. You can see that method two raises the whole greenhouse up, so giving good drainage without further work.

123 *I live on flat land. How can I test if my site needs draining?*

Dig a hole 18in ($\frac{1}{2}$m) deep at the greenhouse site and wait for a period of rain. As soon as the rain stops measure the depth of water at the hole bottom. If any water remains after 24 hours (provided no more rain has fallen) then drainage is required.

124 *Should pipe drains be installed or can some other simpler kind be used?*

Pipes are best, but trenches filled with stone and rubble are cheaper and reasonably effective in all but very wet places. It is common to run the main drain under the central path of the

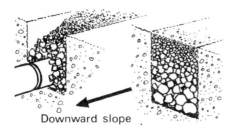

Downward slope

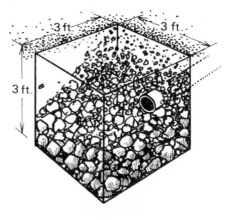

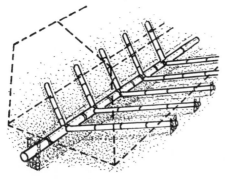

greenhouse drainage it need not be so deep or so large as for outdoor garden drainage—3ft by 3ft by 3ft would probably be adequate, except in heavy clay land that retains water.

greenhouse. Side branch drains can be added in big houses.

125 *How deep should the trenches be dug?*

Take out a main trench sloping from 18in deep to 2ft 6in deep right down the middle of the greenhouse site. Extend the deeper end out into the garden, to carry the drain water clear. Side branches slope down to meet this main.

126 *Where does the water go to from the deeper end?*

On sloping ground of light or medium soil this is no problem. Simply continue the trench along for a few feet to give the water chance to drain away. On flat or heavy ground you must lead the water to a ditch or a soakaway. This is simply a deep hole dug down into any porous subsoil. For

127 *I can't leave such a big hole open in my garden. Can it be covered in some way?*

Certainly. It is usually filled up completely with broken stones, rubble, clinker, etc, which form an open mass into which the water can run freely. Then, in periods between rain, it soaks gradually away into the ground. The drainage trench itself is filled up with similar material, with the pipes, if you are using them, at the bottom.

128 *Are the pipes cemented together?*

No. Arrange them touching, but not fastened. Water enters the drain through these open joints.

129 *Why do we need secondary trenches from the greenhouse sides? Surely one big drain is enough?*

Yes, often, but side drains trap the large amounts of rainwater which cascade off a greenhouse roof.

130 *My greenhouse has gutters and downpipes. Presumably I can best take the side drainage trenches from the bottom of these?*

Yes. It pays too to make a fairly deep hole, filled with rubble, immediately below each downpipe. Otherwise the drain channel immediately beneath may be flooded out every time there is a heavy rainfall, ruining the whole drainage system.

131 *I have been put off buying a greenhouse in case erecting it should prove too difficult. Is this a reasonable worry?*

You need at least two people, fine weather and ample time. Given these, virtually anybody can put up successfully most commercial sectional houses. The bigger the parts, the simpler the erection, naturally, but do not choose a windy day. First though, you must see that the foundation will be sound.

132 *What sort of foundations do greenhouses need?*

Ideally, solid concrete. Subsiding foundations will twist the framework and crack the glass. Concrete cast in place is the most rigid of all. Next, concrete blocks or bricks well cemented. Finally, and only suitable for light greenhouses on dry, firm sites, loose-laid bricks or slabs on rammed soil.

133 *Do all types of greenhouses need such strong foundations?*

The plastic-covered sorts are lighter and will withstand flexing, so they can be erected on plain slabs. With all other sorts, good foundations greatly lengthen the life of the house.

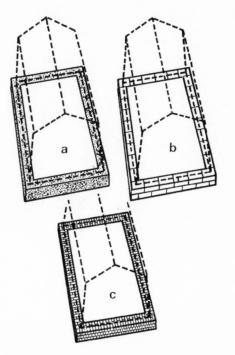

134 *Which would you say was the easiest concrete foundation to make?*

One where you buy precast, shaped concrete base blocks for the particular greenhouse, complete with bolt holes. These can be simply arranged on well-rammed soil and lined up carefully.

135 *Are they cemented together?*

It is useless cementing blocks together, unless you also lay them on a 2–3in thick concrete bed. This makes a much stronger job, well worth doing.

136 *Can I use ordinary bricks or plain concrete blocks instead of the special kinds?*

Yes, but it will mean more work lining them up and preparing them to receive

29

the greenhouse parts. (The special blocks have ready-arranged bolt holes as a rule.) It will cost you less too, especially if you buy used bricks or slabs. Demolition contractors will often sell you the few needed at a very low price.

137 *Is the work easier than making solid concrete foundations?*

Yes. Most people find it easier to work with cemented blocks than with Readymix. You can take your time more, lining up the parts. Though you still need cement, this can be made in small batches as needed. The whole job is less rushed than with ready-mixed concrete. You can also easily knock a few bricks out if they are wrongly placed—not so easy with solid work!

138 *On level land, what is the exact procedure?*

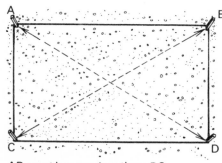

AD must be same length as BC

Peg out with strings the precise shape of the greenhouse, making sure that this is a true rectangle. (Measure across the rectangle diagonally, corner to corner both ways. The two measurements should be exactly the same.) Take some trouble with this until you get the sides, lengths and diagonals equal and accurate.

30

139 *Can I dig foundation trenches with these strings in place?*

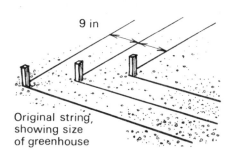

Original string, showing size of greenhouse

No. They are used as a guide for your digging lines. To set these up, stretch two more strings right along one side of your greenhouse. Place these 9in inside and 9in outside the wall line of the greenhouse. Do the same on the other three sides. You now can take out the original string rectangle and use the double marker strings as digging guides. (Make sure the pegs are strong and well secured in place so that if the strings are broken in your digging you can easily replace them.)

140 *What shall I do with the soil removed?*

If this is good topsoil turn it inwards into the greenhouse area. Extra soil depth in the borders will be all to the good. If, however, it is poorish soil, take it away. Do not bank it up near the greenhouse as it may impede drainage. Scatter it thinly over the adjacent garden beds.

141 *How deep should the trenches be?*

On firm, flat land only 6in may be enough. In either very light, sandy soil or heavy clay, dig 12in deep. Ram the trench bottom, then spread a 2in layer of mortar in which to bed the blocks.

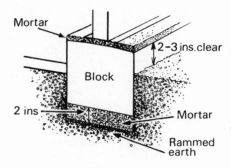

Mortar

2-3 ins.clear

Block

2 ins

Mortar

Rammed earth

142 *What cement mix should I use?*

3 parts of soft builders' sand to 1 part of cement. Do not use concreting sand which is coarser.

143 *What are the main points to watch in laying the blocks?*

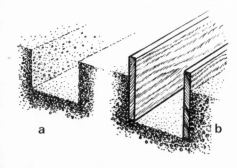

a   b

Getting them perfectly level. Use long boards and strings stretched taut to guide your work. Use mortar that is on the dry side, rather than too wet (water should not run out when the blocks are laid).

144 *Should I make the foundations flush with the soil level?*

No. The house should rest at least 2–3in clear of the soil. As you erect the house, you will spread a further 1in of mortar over the foundations to make a perfect 'bed'.

145 *Can the house be erected as soon as the cement has set?*

Mortar takes several weeks to reach full strength. Let it stand at least ten days. In winter avoid frosty periods. Setting cement is ruined if frozen. Cover all your work with sacking at night. In summer the risk then is of too quick setting. Spread wet sacks over new work for several days.

146 *Since solid concrete foundations are best, how deep should they be?*

This depends upon the site. In firm, flat land you only need to go down about 6in. The foundation trench can be roughly 18in wide and should then, ideally, be filled up solid with coarsely mixed concrete. You can economise on concrete by ramming broken bricks into the concrete as it is laid.

147 *Is it best to use ready-mixed concrete?*

This is very good, perfectly mixed, and only needs shovelling into place. Remember, though, that it must all be put down immediately on delivery. It is cheaper to mix your own concrete, though this saving in cost must be offset against the considerable time mixing takes. By hand, one man might well need two or three weekends to complete even a moderate sized job.

148 *I can hire a power concrete mixer locally. Are these easy to use?*

Yes. Put in the dry materials first: 1 part cement, 2 parts sand, 4 or 5 parts gravel. Mix till they are even in colour. Then add water gradually. Clean the machine really well when finishing work for the day.

31

149 *Is it enough to leave the trenches open for concreting or should I fit extra side supports to hold the concrete in place?*

If you are working in fairly heavy land simply tread the bottom and pack the trench sides firmly. The concrete can be laid directly into it. In softer soils support the wet concrete with rough planks on each side, fitted in the trench.

150 *When making foundations I find it difficult to get a perfectly smooth and level top surface. The bottom edges of my greenhouse are of course straight. How do I fill up the gaps between the building and foundations?*

Just before erection lay a finishing concrete layer 2in thick, smooth it off with trowels and press the structure into it. Alternatively, erect the house and then thoroughly work mortar under and around the bottom of the greenhouse timber work. Bring this 2in up the bottom rails of the greenhouse sides, inside and out.

151 *Surely most greenhouses must be fastened down, using bolts or screws driven into the concrete?*

Yes, this is customary. One method for the skilled is to concrete into the foundations the necessary holding down bolts at the right position. It is extremely difficult to get the bolts accurately in alignment to every hole in the greenhouse structure. It is all too easy to get one $\frac{1}{8}$in out. You then have to alter the holes and this may weaken the structure.

152 *What easier approach is there?*

See if you can separate the bottom rail of the greenhouse complete with its holding down holes. Pass the bolts through these holes then and use the bottom rail to keep them in place until the concrete sets. It should be a perfect fit. A simpler alternative, if you have a power drill, is to leave the concrete smooth and then, when erecting the greenhouse, drill downwards into it for about 3in. You can then fix the greenhouse down with blind ended bolts. These are bolts which drop down into the holes and which, on being tightened, expand to grip the concrete very tightly indeed.

153 *Won't such bolts crack the concrete?*

Only if you are too hasty and fail to allow the concrete time to go hard before fixing them.

154 *How are sectional greenhouses erected?*

This will differ with the make and unfortunately some manufacturers' instructions are far from adequate! They may be too complicated or too sparse—or indeed actually wrong! However, the principles of bolting together the sections are easy to see at a glance and there is not usually much problem. This is especially true with wooden greenhouses which come in largish frames with ready drilled bolt holes. The thing to watch is that you get the right pieces in the right places. Check this patiently. It is sometimes possible to reverse the positions of some parts. Sections may look alike but may still differ in the position of one or two of the bolt holes.

155 *Are aluminium greenhouses more difficult to erect?*

This again depends on the type.

Usually they are fairly easy to deal with, especially if they come in large sections. Some sorts though, especially the circular kinds, may be supplied like a giant construction set, broken down into dozens of individual strips of metal. They can be complicated to understand at first. Allow yourself plenty of time to sort out the parts beforehand, and do not go too hastily at the job. Make sure at each stage that the parts fit together in accordance with the diagrams supplied. Many bits look similar. Never force a fit—this usually means a mistake!

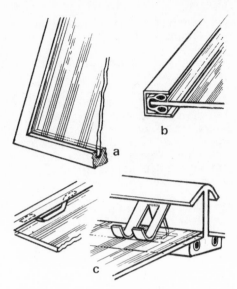

156 What problems are there with fitting the glass?

The most likely is simply dropping or banging the glass! Cuts can be largely avoided by wearing extremely tough gloves but it is very easy to knock the corner off a glass pane, or to accidentally twist and crack one. Again, never try to force a fit. If the panes do not lie flat, it means the frame is twisted.

157 What about the different glass fixing methods; are these difficult to do?

No. In wood there is often a slot within which the panes can be slipped quite easily. There may be a retaining plastic strip which again is usually no problem to fix. There are various patent types of clip which can be used with wood and aluminium. Study the instructions to get the general hang of the method before starting. A pair of pliers and one or two screwdrivers may be useful in getting the clips to fit solidly into place. The main hazard is losing the clips especially if you are working near grass or tall weeds. Putty is not used in most cases. Only old,

traditionally built houses use putty these days.

Greenhouse Heating and Lighting – Soil Warming – Power Supplies – Temperature Checking and Control

158 Is it vital to have heating in a greenhouse?

No, but it does vastly increase the use it will get. Cold houses will soon drop to outdoor temperatures in winter so there are long periods when it is of little real service.

159 I have read, though, that cool houses will grow all sorts of things.

Cool has particular meaning in greenhouse work. It usually denotes a greenhouse which has no form of artificial heating during the summer. All the heat comes from the sun. Any heat used during the colder parts of the year is just to keep frost out. The

33

minimum temperature then may be only around 45°F (7.2°C).

160 *What use is such a degree of warmth in winter?*

Mainly for storing sensitive plant material such as half-hardy garden plants, tubers, etc. In food growing, though, even this small amount of heat can help in starting off early crops of tomatoes and, of course, for the forcing of winter vegetables.

161 *What sort of plants require the most heat?*

None of the food plants, fortunately. A hothouse will usually be kept above 65°F (18.3°C) and is mainly used for tropical flowering plants, orchids, etc.

162 *But surely tomatoes and cucumbers in particular require a considerable amount of heat?*

Yes. These are next down the list. The night temperature should never fall below 55°F (12.8°C). With this heat, once these food plants have been taken away you can continue to use the greenhouse for pot plants, propagation and winter flowers as well as the usual forcing of vegetables.

163 *I am a newcomer to greenhouse work. What level of heating should I try to achieve?*

Start simply. It is all too easy to spend far too much, too early, before you really know what your aims are. You can get along fine for the first couple of years without summer heating and only a small horticultural oil heater to keep the frost out in the winter. With this simple equipment you can gain experience and still grow valuable crops.

164 *What are the main disadvantages of this approach?*

You may have to buy in some of your early plants, and your crops will not be so early.

165 *We have mild winters, with frost only in midwinter for odd weeks. Surely a cold house will serve for us?*

Perhaps so, especially if you buy in your plants. Cold houses can then catch up with medium heat greenhouses and give much the same crops.

166 *There seem to be many makes and types of oil heaters. Which should I choose?*

The simplest, free-standing, and of a kind that can later, if you install better heating, be used in the house, garage or workshop. There is little to choose between makes, but do make certain that the heater is for greenhouses. Ordinary types may give off poisonous fumes.

167 *How much fuel will I use per week?*

Nobody can answer this. It depends on:

1 The interior heat you maintain
2 The outside temperature
3 The efficiency of the heater itself
4 The care you take in keeping the burners trimmed
5 The soundness of the greenhouse structure
6 The prevailing wind strength, humidity and rainfall.

All you can say is that it is likely to be the cheapest heat.

168 *Would such a simple arrangement be suitable for greenhouses in the North?*

The farther north you get the less useful is the cool house. If you rely solely on summer sun you are likely to have only a short growing season, with reduced crops, so heating must start early in autumn and be kept on late into spring.

169 *What about in the far South, where we are blessed with warm springs and have little frost in winter?*

If the winters are as mild as all that, you may hardly need a greenhouse at all! Indeed, ventilation may be more of a problem than heating. Remember the aim of a greenhouse is to transform a moderately warm, short season into a longer, even warmer one, keeping out frost and cold winds and providing the maximum light. If you already have these blessings outdoors there is not much need to provide them artificially!

170 *If I don't have any heating at all what is the main risk I face?*

You may start off plants in early spring as the weather warms up and then meet a sudden, sharp frost. Without some form of heating, this will destroy the young seedlings. Growth later too, will be slow in cold weather. At the other end of the season, early frosts or cold winds can check the plants' growth prematurely. Finally, plants stored over winter in an unheated greenhouse might as well be outdoors since the temperature in long cold spells will drop well below freezing.

171 *Why do gardeners often install more powerful and expensive heating?*

By having more controllable heat for a longer period of the year you can extend dramatically the seasons at which your food supplies are available. You get them both earlier and later. You can also improve the quality of the crops by controlling exactly the amount of heat they get at various times. The weight produced will also be greater since the plants will grow on more steadily and fruitfully.

172 *But surely heating costs are very high these days. Is it really worth it financially?*

In a well run house, the costs are far lower than the value of produce raised.

173 *Though the cheapest type of greenhouse heater seems to be the ordinary paraffin stove, it must have some disadvantage?*

Yes. The amount of attention it needs. You have to light it and put it out, or lower its heat output, with changing weather and time of day.

174 *Surely this cannot be very often during the week?*

For most efficient use of fuel, and the benefit of plants, there may be temperature changes two or three times a day, to cope with cool evenings and mornings or bright sun at midday. If you fail to turn the heat up at night you can lose your plants through frost, and too hot conditions in midday can cause them to collapse, or at least would waste a lot of fuel. If you can actually give detailed attention, they are very efficient in overall terms, bearing in mind their low capital costs.

175 *Surely you need the same sort of regular attention to solid fuel boilers?*

Yes, but to a much lesser extent. Nowadays, most boilers can be filled by semi-automatic action. The heat output is controlled by a thermostat. This sort, though fairly expensive, will look after themselves for long periods.

176 *Most oil fuelled systems are automatic I believe?*

Yes, but not all. If there is no circulation pump, regular attention will be required. Gas is sometimes used instead of oil, and needs practically no attention at all.

177 *What is the most automatic of heating systems?*

Electricity. It is also the easiest to install and control. It is simple to alter the heat setting as often as you wish.

178 *How effective are storage heaters in using electricity?*

The usual kinds are not very effective since the heat output during the day is not controlled by the warmth of the day but by the temperature of the preceding night. A cold night will have caused the heater to warm up well and next day the build up of heat must be released, even if the day is quite sunny. There will always be more

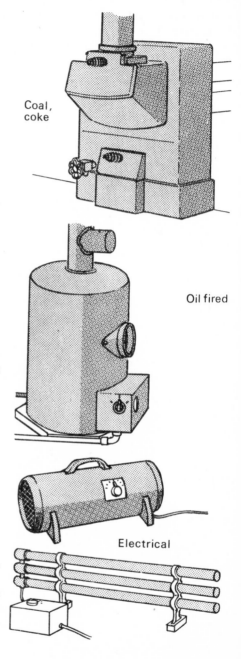

Coal, coke

Oil fired

Electrical

heat released after a cold night than after a warm night.

179 *Is there no way of controlling this?*

There are systems available and you should consult the electricity board for the latest developments, especially since the rules relating to offpeak heating charges and the relative prices of offpeak power may change.

180 *What are the disadvantages of using electricity for heating?*

Electricity has usually the highest cost for its heat output, and power cuts are always possible.

181 *What is the next simplest in operation?*

A fully automatic oil or gas-fired system with small bore pipes and a circulating pump.

182 *Can I convert an existing solid fuel system to oil or gas, in an old but sound greenhouse?*

Yes, either by fitting new burners in the existing boiler, or installing a new boiler.

183 *Is it feasible too, to make it into a fully automatic, pumped circulation system?*

Not always. If, as is likely, your existing system has large diameter cast iron piping it is very hard to ensure safe installation of a pumped system. As the pumps cut in, high pressures are generated for a short time and the old-fashioned joints will not withstand this very well.

184 *With a lean-to house, could I not simply extend the house central*

heating into it?

This depends entirely upon your system. You might find it extremely difficult to bore through an outside wall to let pipes through. Also, some house heat control systems turn the entire boiler off from time to time, such as overnight, just when heat may be needed by the greenhouse.

185 *So it would only really be possible where the boiler is working day and night?*

Yes, and this might affect the efficiency of the house heating. Do not try this sort of modification yourself without having the plans carefully checked by a heating engineer.

186 *When you install a new greenhouse boiler, where should it be placed?*

On the side away from prevailing winds so that you don't get fumes blowing into the greenhouse.

187 *Is it best to mount heating pipes on the greenhouse frame or on separate supports?*

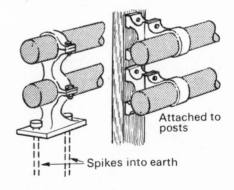

Attached to posts

Spikes into earth

Always use separate supports where possible or at least reinforce the greenhouse frame at the positions of attachment. Many amateur greenhouses are carefully designed to use the least possible amount of timber (so reducing their cost). Adding the weight of a heavy heater pipe installation may be too much for the structure in the long run.

188 *How can I design the actual heating installation, to ensure good water circulation, suitable oil supply pipes, ventilation, etc?*

It is best not to do so. Most suppliers will give you free advice or even designs for your specific needs. Unskilled layout may easily produce odd siphoning effects, air locks, etc, which either make the heater work poorly or use a lot of fuel. The design of heating systems, especially piped types, is a skilled job best left to experts. Electric systems are a little easier to plan, since the heat output of the units is standardised and there are no circulation problems. The makers of the equipment are glad to give assistance, as also are the electricity boards.

189 *Are hot air systems effective for greenhouses?*

Yes, though most are used commercially. There are excellent fan-driven electric hot air circulators available. Their installation cost is very small, since they only need a power point.

190 *How shall I install the power cable from the house mains to the greenhouse?*

You shouldn't! Unless you are a skilled electrician, you are likely to rig up an installation that is both dangerous and illegal. Get a qualified electrician to do

38

this vital work. To keep this cost down though, a lot of time may be saved if you yourself take out and refill the necessary trench for an underground cable. Apart from that, there is little you can do. Remember, though, that as a bonus you will get electric lighting too to provide working illumination for winter or dark evenings. Light can also (when you gain experience) be provided for the plants themselves. They need light to develop and many commercial growers use powerful illumination to extend the day and provide extra growth. You will get power too for automatic equipment, pumps, fans, etc.

191 *Does greenhouse wiring call for special fittings of any kind?*

Yes. Ensure that all parts used are completely waterproof. Never use ordinary domestic fittings.

192 *What is soil warming?*

This usually means using electric cables arranged underneath the soil to keep it warm. It can mean any other form of heating, such as steel pipes under the soil, for the same purpose. It is dangerous to have high voltage electric wires underneath the soil in a greenhouse or even on a potting bench, so all installations have a transformer to reduce the voltage to a safe level.

193 *What is the advantage of this system?*

Germination of seeds and growth of plants is always quicker when the soil is warm. It may take a long time for the temperature of border soil to rise in spring. Soil heating can speed this up immensely. It is not so wasteful as other forms of heating because all the electricity is actually used, and you can control the amount you give by a simple form of time clock device and thermostat.

194 *Does the heat have to be on all day?*

No, 8 hours is usually quite adequate. The soil temperature will be raised during this time and will not drop very rapidly. It is best to give heat for several shorter periods, say 2 hours, 4 times a day, rather than a continuous 8 hours.

195 *How can I cut heating costs in my greenhouse?*

Try lining it with polythene. This reduces heat loss through the glass quite considerably, so making your heating system more efficient. Block up draughts, especially around the door. Do not maintain unnecessarily high temperatures. Erect shelter from cold winds.

196 *How can polythene linings be fixed in metal greenhouses?*

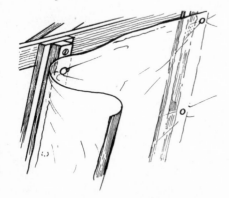

This is not easy. You must first put up a simple, lightweight wooden frame inside the greenhouse structure. 1in sq

softwood lightly bolted to holes drilled through the aluminium framing will do (it is quite easy to drill). The polythene itself is then tacked to the wood.

197 *I have found that after putting up polythene, condensation greatly increased. Will this affect my plants?*

A few plants dislike high humidity but this can usually be controlled by a slight increase in ventilation. Many others, such as cucumbers, actively prefer a steamy atmosphere and high heat. For them polythene is a definite advantage.

198 *I have seen gardeners cover their greenhouse plants with newspapers on cold evenings. Is this very helpful?*

Two or three layers of newspapers loosely spaced can give considerable protection, even in unheated houses and frames.

199 *In checking the temperature of my greenhouse I find quite marked differences from place to place. I find it difficult to tell which reading to use in deciding whether the house is too hot or too cool.*

It is not always easy to find a position which will reflect accurately the temperature of the greenhouse from the point of view of the plant. For example, if a thermometer is placed in full sun it will obviously get much hotter than in shaded parts of the greenhouse. Even the presence of a nearby water tank can alter the temperature by a few degrees. In other places low readings may arise if the thermometer is sited near a draught from a ventilator, a hole or crack in the glass or framing.

ADVANTAGES	DISADVANTAGES

PARAFFIN STOVES

Cheap to buy	Need fairly frequent attention
Easy to install	May smell
Useable elsewhere later	A small fire risk
Low cost fuel	

SOLID FUEL

May be automatically controlled	Rather high installation cost
Relatively cheap fuel	May have slow response to
Reliable, permanent system	temperature changes
	Heavy fuel that must be hand-loaded

OIL FIRED HEATERS

Easily automated completely	High initial costs
Reliable permanent system	Fuel rising steadily in price
Quickly responsive to temperature changes	
No fuel transportation	

ELECTRICITY

Comparatively low capital costs	Rising power cost
Easily installed and extended (apart from power supply)	Small electric shock risk, especially if installed by amateurs
Complete, accurate control	Possible power cuts or failures
Very efficient use of power supplied	

GAS

Moderate capital cost, especially if added to an existing boiler, fairly near to the house	Some fume hazard in poor installations. **Must** be professionally checked for fire and explosion risks
Efficient use of fuel	
Needs little attention	
Very clean-burning	

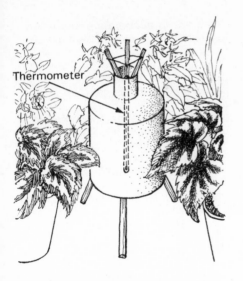

Thermometer

201 *What can be done to check the temperature accurately?*

Get a white plastic container about 6in in diameter and cut off its base so that you have a cylinder. Support this on a tripod of sticks and suspend the thermometer inside. Arrange this apparatus amongst the plants themselves and at their level. The shield will prevent draughts affecting the reading and also keep the instrument from the direct rays of the sun. (If you can temporarily fit up a domestic fan some distance away to give a gentle air flow through the protecting cylinder so much the better.)

202 *Where should I put this apparatus?*

First, place it for half-hour stretches in different parts of the greenhouse and record the readings. If any places register much higher or lower than average, avoid these spots and finally leave the thermometer (in its protective cylinder) at a place that reads nearest to the average. Your heating thermostat, if you have one, should be similarly placed.

203 *So I should take several readings, find the average, and then site the thermometer and thermostat at the place with a reading nearest to that amount?*

Correct. Suppose that you took four readings, one of which gave 60°F (15.6°C), one 30°F (−1.1°C), and two of them 40°F (4.4°C). The average of this amount is 42°F (5.6°C), so place the thermometer in either of the two places which recorded 40°F (4.4°C). This is likely to give you a good average reading at all times.

Greenhouse Equipment for Ventilation, Watering, Working

204 *It seems a strange thing to pay for greenhouse heating and then to open windows to let the nice warm air out! How important actually is ventilation?*

Extremely important. Without it the plants will die. Like animals, plants require a constant flow of fresh air to be able to breathe.

205 *I always thought ventilation was to reduce humidity and condensation inside greenhouses?*

This is one of its effects since too moist conditions may encourage fungus disease. But fresh air entry is just as important.

206 *Opening and closing ventilators is quite a chore. How automatic can this be made?*

Totally automatic by electronic means if you can afford the cost. Fortunately

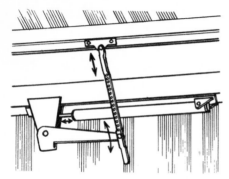

difference in temperature and where this is not great it might be quite slow. Fans are quicker.

209 *Are these the domestic fans such as are fitted in kitchens?*

No. These create too concentrated a draught for plants. It is far better to install horticultural types with very large fans. These suck the air powerfully but relatively slowly.

though, many simpler, semi-automatic mechanisms are quite cheap and require no electric power. They operate by the expansion of chemical grease. A simple cylinder system is screwed to the ventilator and the nearby greenhouse framing. When the temperature rises the contents of the cylinder expand and push open the ventilator. As the greenhouse cools the chemical contracts and pulls the ventilator shut again.

210 *You tell us to put greenhouses in a sunny position. Why then do many gardeners provide shading blinds?*

Almost any greenhouses may become over-hot in summer and if this is coupled with high humidity you can get attacks of disease. Too much light is also bad for starting off vegetable seedlings in a warm spring. In each case shading is not merely desirable but almost vital.

207 *What other automatic types are there?*

Electrical types where various motors or magnets are used to control opening and shutting at a particular temperature setting. These are easier to set to control the overall temperature of a greenhouse within close limits.

211 *How is shading best provided?*

The most permanent, easily adjusted and attractive forms of shading are

208 *I have seen greenhouses fitted with fans for ventilation. Are these better than ordinary ventilators?*

They are more positive in action. Ordinary ventilators depend for the release of air on the fact that warm air rises. This is why vents are commonly placed high up. Then cold air is sucked in from other ventilators nearer the bottom. The speed at which this takes place depends upon the

slatted or treated cloth blinds on rollers up the sunward sides of the greenhouse. Many gardeners though simply spray their greenhouses with whitewash. It is a cheap method, and quite effective. It is usually a simple mix of lime and water, though there are proprietary sprays as well. It usually weathers off with the rains of autumn. Any remaining should brush off fairly readily in winter with a hose-pipe and sweeping brush.

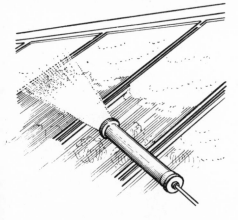

212 What is the most effective method of watering greenhouse plants?

A watering can. A highly skilled grower is able to judge his plants' requirements almost exactly by their appearance and can give individual attention to each.

213 Is can watering also best for the newcomer?

It is certainly the simplest and cheapest but takes more effort than using a hose-pipe. Can water, too, may be warmer if supplies are dipped from a greenhouse storage tank. This is more important in winter when the greenhouse (and the plants' roots)

may be quite warm but the pipes outside underground very cold indeed.

214 What sort of labour-saving watering systems are available?

A hose-pipe with a controllable nozzle end tap is the obvious, cheapest answer. There are also semi-automatic systems than can be fairly easily fixed up with perforated hose-pipes laid over the growing borders so that the spray falls near the plants. Then all that is needed is to turn on the tap at the appropriate time for every plant to get its share.

215 What is capillary watering?

A system for watering pot plants standing on a 2in bed of coarsish sand.

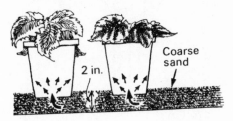

2 in.

Coarse sand

43

Water is pumped up into the sand and the pots absorb it through their drainholes. Before the sand bed is dried up completely a valve opens to supply more water.

216 *Is the system used much for food growing?*

Not a lot, though it is helpful with ring-grown tomatoes. These still require other means of watering and spraying.

217 *How do I water plants in a cold house in winter when frost is about?*

Be very sparing of water and do it in the morning. The house interior must be dry before frost starts at night.

218 *What sort of working benches are best in greenhouses?*

For food growing, benches are not so vital as for pot plants, etc. Still, most of us grow a variety of plants so it is useful to have at least a small bench. Make it 32in high, 36in wide and as long as is convenient. It is simplest to make the framing in wood, though the actual working top may be of asbestos or even corrugated iron, covered in sand.

219 *I have seen many greenhouse benches that are slatted, with gaps between the wood strips. What is the advantage of this?*

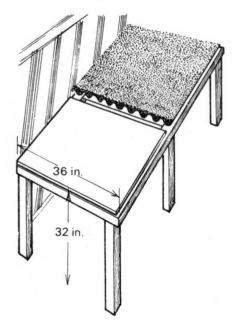

36 in.

32 in.

This type is very good for growing pot plants on because air can rise between the slats. For food growing work the solid bench is better. Much of the bench work for good growing consists of filling boxes with compost and a solid working surface is obviously essential. Slatted shelves, however, higher up the greenhouse walls, are useful for standing the boxes as the seeds germinate.

220 *What is a propagating case?*

An enclosure like a garden frame, but inside the greenhouse, in which a

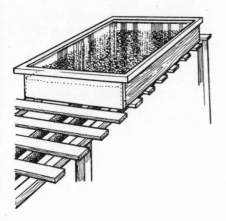

Shelves, both on end walls and high up near the glass (for developing seedlings). A small cupboard with a lock for weedkillers and pesticides.

222 *Will I need special tools for greenhouse food growing?*

Besides the usual watering can, spade, fork and rake, you may buy a good water-spray apparatus (for overhead water syringing) and an insecticide sprayer. Keep these separate. A sharp knife is handy. A horticultural thermometer is almost essential.

higher temperature can be maintained for seed germination or striking cuttings. A useful tool, especially if you grow flowers as well as food. You can make one yourself. Indeed, a rectangle of timber, 6–7in deep, with an old picture frame placed over, will do quite well. Place a 4in thick layer of moist peat inside. If possible, provide bottom heat by building the case over pipes.

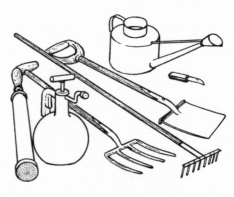

Greenhouse Maintenance

223 *How much maintenance do greenhouses require?*

This depends on the material. Red cedar will not normally rot, so in theory you can leave it without any attention. In practice, the appearance of the greenhouse will change from a rich red to a silvery grey. You can keep the red colour by painting the wood with a light oil. This does not take very long.

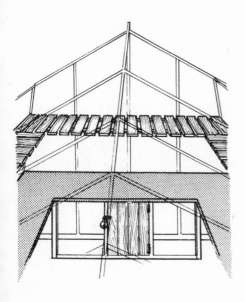

45

224 *What about hardwood greenhouses?*

These again require practically no maintenance, though it is customary to treat them with linseed oil every year or two.

225 *Preserved softwood presumably does need painting at some time?*

Pressure-preserved softwood lasts for some years without further treatment. After about four years you can apply a liquid wood preservative, preferably of a kind recommended by the original greenhouse manufacturer. This will reinforce the original preservative and give it a new lease of life. Ordinary softwood houses that have not been pressure treated do require painting nearly every year. Use any good outdoor-grade oil paint.

226 *When is the best time of the year to do this painting?*

Probably in the very late summer whilst working conditions are still pleasant and you are likely to do a fairly good job. This means that during the winter you will have the protection of a new coat of paint just when it is most needed.

227 *The glass in my old greenhouse is held in by putty. Should I paint over the putty?*

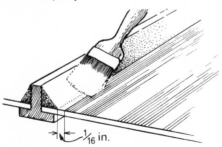

Always paint over putty, provided this is sound, and let the paint extend about $\frac{1}{16}$ in on to the glass itself. This helps to seal the edge of the putty against water.

228 *Can I use creosote, which is a very cheap and powerful wood preservative, on greenhouses and frames?*

Never. Creosote is very poisonous to many plants and the fumes that it gives off can severely injure greenhouse plants.

229 *Should I remove the glass before painting?*

If you can spare the time and are used to handling glass this is much better. It speeds up the painting work tremendously and enables you to paint the pieces directly touching the glass which would otherwise not be reached. Do a little at a time. Take out a few panes and paint the frames with rapid drying paint and slide the glass back into place as soon as this is touch dry. (Established greenhouses depend for their strength partly on the glass itself. If you remove it all at once it might be difficult to fit it back again.)

230 *My glass gets dirty because we live fairly near a large town. What shall I use to clean it with?*

You can buy special glass cleaning fluids but a cheaper method is to dissolve 2lb of oxalic acid in a large can of water. Spray this over the glass and hose it off later. If the glass has a heavy, greenish discolouration at the edges you will probably have to scrape it away. Some gardeners use tar oil winter wash (as for fruit trees) to kill moss of this kind.

231 *When a greenhouse has a solid wall, what colour should the inside be painted?*

White, because white reflects the most light. The tall inside wall of a lean-to should always be kept especially clean and white. This makes quite a considerable difference to the plants.

232 *What other maintenance will be needed, if painting is properly done?*

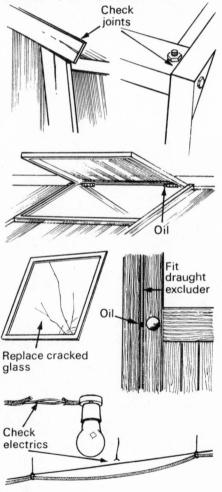

Check joints

Oil

Fit draught excluder

Oil

Replace cracked glass

Check electrics

Annually, and after strong winds, take a careful look at all the wood (or metal) joints, to make sure they are not working loose. Tighten screws and erection bolts. Oil and grease hinges and catches. Replace cracked panes. Check doors for fit and fix draught excluder strips if necessary, to save heat. Turn off mains power at the mains switch and check electric fittings for security and cables for chafing or cracking. Look at any overhead cable and its supporting wire for signs of weakness at supports, etc. See to routine cleaning of heating equipment. Replace cracked putty. Look for draughts and seal up with materials like self-adhesive bitumen strips, sealing adhesives, etc.

Soils, Sterilisation, Weed Control and Manures

233 *What type of soil is best for greenhouse borders?*

Most kinds will do. You can usually accept the soil you already have in your garden. Almost any soil can be improved to a fertile growing medium, no matter how it starts out. Of course some are easier than others! Very broadly there are light soils, consisting largely of sand and silt with very little clay; medium soils, which have more or less equal proportions of sand, silt, clay; and heavy soils, largely clay with very little sand.

234 *How is it that such different types of soil can be modified so as to be suitable for greenhouse work?*

Soils differ mainly in the proportions of sand, silt, clay and organic material that they contain. Due to the small soil area of a greenhouse it is not too difficult to change these proportions.

47

Sandy, light soil is easiest to dig, but medium soils give the best results, whilst heavy soils need special treatment to lighten them.

235 *What is the disadvantage of light soils?*

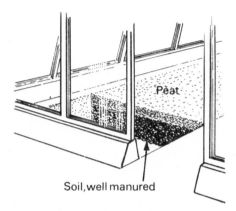

Soil, well manured

They do not hold on to plant food well. They drain rapidly and the water carries away the soil chemicals. To improve this, add more 'body' with clay or bulky organic materials of a heavy kind such as farmyard manure. This will make the overall texture heavier. Heavy dressings of peat (up to 4in thick) can also be used to improve water-retaining characteristics.

236 *Will I need so much farm manure?*

You are unlikely these days to have too much. A barrow-load per square yard is fine. Make sure, though, that it has been stacked outside, and turned at intervals, for at least six weeks before bringing it in.

237 *Is rotted compost from last year as good as farm manure?*

It can be, provided it is well rotted down, and the right chemicals added. Most domestic compost, though, is less fertile than farm manure.

238 *What about medium soil? Presumably this requires very little attention.*

There is an infinite gradation of soil textures from light right through to heavy. A medium soil may be on the light side or on the heavy side. In the middle of the range its texture may need little improvement. Of course you will still have to deal with its chemical content, which we discuss later on.

239 *How can I improve very heavy clay soils?*

This may be more difficult. It is not only a question of introducing sand and peat to open up the soil texture. The greenhouse will be surrounded by heavy clay outside and this will impede drainage and may keep the greenhouse waterlogged. First-class drainage is essential in such cases.

240 *I have been told that farmyard manure improves heavy clay, yet you say above it is used to improve light sand. Which is correct?*

Both. Farmyard manure is the most versatile of soil improvement materials. Its coarse texture opens out clay and improves drainage, besides giving extra organic matter. In sand, its action is to provide a spongy water reserve, binding the loose sand particles together. Applying it does not increase water drainage through sand since this is already so high.

241 *There are several soil conditioners advertised which are* *supposed to transform heavy land into good medium soil without effort. Are these worthwhile?*

They can be, especially on such small areas as greenhouse borders. They must, though, be correctly applied, in accordance with the manufacturers' instructions. You can then expect a considerable improvement. It is usually also desirable to treat the land immediately outside the greenhouse as well, so the cost of this should be considered too.

242 *Once the texture of the soil is improved, how can I check whether its chemical food content is adequate?*

Send away samples of soil for analysis. Your local council may run a soil analytical service and several major fertiliser companies do the same. These analyses will tell you roughly how much lime and other chemicals are present in the soil and what treatment is needed to give an adequate balance of plant food. You can even do this test yourself, by buying simple soil testing kits which in most cases give reasonably good results.

243 *What do such kits tell me?*

The simplest sort simply measure the acidity of the soil. They then tell you how much lime you should apply. Cover a pinch of soil with water, and compare the colour of the resulting liquid with a chart. This will tell you roughly how much lime the soil needs.

244 *A soil analysis referred to the 'pH' number. What is this?*

A measure of acidity. A pH of 7.0 is neutral, neither acid nor alkaline. Lower numbers mean increasing

acidity. Higher numbers mean the soil is alkaline.

245 *What about tests for fertiliser needs?*

These are rather less accurate and detailed, though you can get a good indication of any serious deficiency by using them. The method is the same, checking the colour of a liquid against a provided chart. It is vital to follow the instructions carefully.

246 *I did such tests on my garden and found widely different results from different parts. Is this normal?*

Yes. In mature gardens there may be parts that have in the past been used used for compost or manure stacks, rose beds, vegetable patches, etc. Some will have been heavily fertilised and will have quite a different chemical content from areas under old paths or lawns. In new gardens, lime and cement will often have been stacked or spilt during building and this will affect the chemical analysis.

247 *Is it always vital to have soil analysed?*

Not if the soil has been growing reasonable vegetable or flower crops —or even a healthy batch of weeds! Any such growth indicates that it is capable of producing plant food in reasonable quantities.

248 *What if my soil is alkaline, as in chalk areas? How can I make it more acid?*

This is much more difficult. In fact, you would usually find it simplest to replace the soil. This is not worthwhile in an outside garden but might certainly be done in the small area of a greenhouse. It is so beneficial to have a slightly acid soil that it is worth the labour of digging away all the alkaline soil and replacing it with a good, medium loam.

249 *Where would I obtain such soil?*

You will have to buy it. A nurseryman might be able to advise on local suppliers. It can be fairly expensive. However, compared to the cost of the greenhouse, it is small, and will bring great advantages over the following years.

250 *How much soil will I need to order?*

Very roughly, 1 ton is equal to 1 cubic yard. Measure the border areas of your greenhouse (in square feet) and divide this by 18. This will give you the answer in tons of soil needed to provide a depth of 18in. For example: a border 12ft by 3ft equals 36 sq ft, divided by 18, needs 2 tons. Since you have to remove this volume of old soil it may turn out quite a major job, but it is usually a once and for all undertaking.

251 *Can I save work by raising the borders with the fresh soil, say for 6in, and resting this against the bottom of the greenhouse glass?*

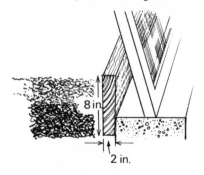

8 in

2 in.

No. The roots would soon reach the alkaline soil below. In other soils though, increasing the depth by raising ridged borders is beneficial, but always provide a raised support for it next to the glass, or you will have trouble later. An 8in by 2in rough wooden batten will serve for years.

252 *Some gardeners change the soil in their greenhouse every year. Is this to reduce risk of disease?*

Yes. Various fungus and virus diseases have a dormant period each winter, living on in the soil. By removing this and replacing it with fresh soil the chance of attack is much reduced. This means a lot of work, and much the same result can be obtained by partial sterilisation by steam or chemical. This is effective but must be carefully done.

253 *It seems odd to sterilise soil when you want plants to grow in it?*

The full phrase is partial sterilisation. Not everything living in the soil is destroyed. If this did take place the soil would not grow any plants at all! Newly erected greenhouses with fresh, fertile soil may not need sterilisation for a year or more.

254 *I suppose plants grown in sterilised soil are also less likely to catch disease?*

Funnily enough, no. The harmful bacteria removed by partial sterilisation are not only those that cause disease. Indeed, some of them may actually be involved in the defence of plants. Disease organisms may actually develop more easily in sterilised soil but they have to come from outside.

255 *Which sterilisation method is best for the amateur?*

Chemical sterilisation, though you must take care to follow the makers' instructions. The chemicals used can be poisonous. One that is effective and reasonably safe is metham sodium, manufactured in powder form, which is very simple to work with. When the chemicals are applied to the soil, as directed, a gas is developed which is poisonous to harmful bacteria. (It is also very harmful at this stage to growing plants and remains so for anything up to five or six weeks.)

256 *Is the soil treated in boxes, heaps or in the borders themselves?*

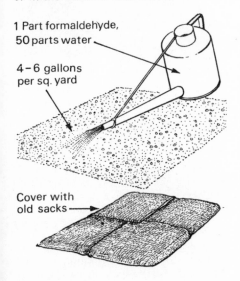

1 Part formaldehyde, 50 parts water

4 – 6 gallons per sq. yard

Cover with old sacks

In any of these ways. Instructions are given with the material. Formalin (formaldehyde) has also been used for many years and is quite effective. You need 1 part of formaldehyde dissolved in 50 parts of water and applied at 4–6 gal per square yard.

Once this has been done, cover the soil with old sacks.

257 *Are there any simpler methods for amateur use where poisonous chemicals are not needed?*

Hot water sterilisation can be used, especially for small quantities. This is done by raising the soil temperature by the use of steam or water for 10 minutes. The aim is to heat the soil to about 170°F (76.7°C). Spread soil in thin layers on benches or alternatively suspend a bag of soil in porous cloth above boiling water. The steam penetrates the soil to raise the temperature as required.

258 *What about bigger amounts?*

It all depends if you have a big enough container to house the boiling water. The old-fashioned domestic copper was ideal. In this a large volume of water could be brought to the boil and a metal bucket filled with soil suspended in it. It was kept there for half an hour till the soil was thoroughly heated. You can also bake soil dry on an improvised grill but this

51

is an extremely delicate operation. It is all too easy to 'cook' it too hard. There are also specially made electric sterilisers which are really rather expensive for amateur use.

259 *How soon after heat treatment can I plant the greenhouse?*

About fourteen days.

260 *Does sterilisation reduce attack by pests as well as by disease?*

The root eelworm can be a great trouble with tomatoes.' Both steam and metham sodium will tackle this but formalin will not. The treatment also kills off most common weed seeds. Virus diseases are much more resistant. Damping off and wilt diseases are quite well controlled by steam, metham sodium or formaldehyde.

261 *What about weed seeds, etc?*

There should be no difficulty with weeds. In such a small area you should be able to clear them away pretty thoroughly.

262 *What about actual full-grown weeds? Our new garden is chock full of huge, tough old nettles, docks and other deeply rooting and spreading weeds!*

To avoid having a continual fight with these over the years, it is best to deal with them early, clearing them by really thorough digging, weedkillers or both.

263 *If I use weedkillers, surely these may poison the soil?*

Sodium chlorate is an inflammable but cheap, powerful killer of all plants, but takes six months to wash clear out-of-doors. Many others, though more expensive, are based on specialised and often poisonous chemicals such as paraquat, and treated soil is usable practically at once. Follow the makers' instructions *exactly!*

264 *What type of cultivation is best for greenhouse borders?*

Remove top 10 inches of soil

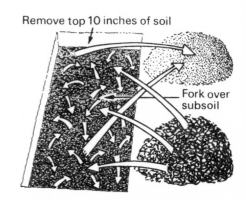

Fork over subsoil

This depends on the soil. Heavy soil needs deeper cultivation than sandy. With a new greenhouse, double digging is best done before erection. This involves breaking up the subsoil (the infertile layers of soil below the first 10in). Start by excavating the top 10in of soil and barrowing it away to a stack. This will expose the less fertile subsoil, often of a different colour. Fork this subsoil over deeply, the main aim being to open up its texture to make perfect drainage. At the same time, dig in quantities of farmyard manure, with more reserved for when you replace the top 10in of soil.

265 *How can I deep dig soil without such complete removal?*

Take out a trench 1ft deep and 1ft wide across one end of the

52

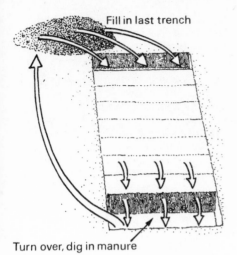

Fill in last trench

Turn over, dig in manure

greenhouse. Wheelbarrow the top soil to the other end. Turn over the subsoil at the bottom of this trench, working in manure, and then dig the topsoil from the adjacent strip and throw it forward on to the top of the subsoil you have already dug. This will expose more subsoil to be turned over in its turn. At the end of the greenhouse the topsoil you removed first will go to fill up the very last trench.

266 *How much farmyard manure should be used?*

At least a barrow-load for every 10–12 yd. If you cannot get manure use peat, leafmould or well prepared garden compost (rotted down garden refuse).

267 *During their lives, most cultivated plants seem to need added fertilisers. Are natural manures better than chemicals?*

Plants only live on chemicals. They convert the so-called 'natural' fertilisers to these before they can absorb them.

268 *Why is there all the argument then about artificial or natural fertilisers?*

It is easy to overdo chemical fertilising and cause disastrous results. Excessive raw fertilisers can destroy the structure of the soil, changing its texture, and drastically reducing its fertility. This happened to such an extent outdoors, especially in America, that there was a reaction against chemical fertilisers.

269 *What is the true position at present?*

As with most things, moderation is essential. Artificial fertilisers are widely used in greenhouses because you can control very precisely the amount you give. With farmyard manures the quality is variable, the amount of chemicals they contain differs, and this makes it hard to give accurately controlled feeding.

270 *Some gardeners claim not to use soil at all. How is this possible?*

Soil is required by the plant for two purposes. To give an effective anchorage for its roots and to store chemicals for food. The first can be given by any sort of medium such as vermiculite, sand or peat, none of which contain plant food to any extent. Once the support is given, pure plant food chemicals can be applied as liquids or powders at carefully controlled rates. Soil then is not needed.

271 *Isn't this a very complicated, artificial business?*

Not really, because mixtures can be fairly easily made up in the form of soilless composts which give balanced

53

feeding of plants, and strong root anchorage.

272 *The question of fertilisers seems to be considered to be more important in greenhouses than out-of-doors. Why is this?*

There is only a limited amount of soil in a greenhouse. Because of this, comparatively soon a particular chemical may be completely removed, drastically affecting the plants' growth. A correct balance of chemicals must be maintained at all times.

273 *Do all plants require exactly the same chemicals?*

Not precisely, but there is a general chemical balance to which most plants will respond. In the intensive growing conditions of a greenhouse, however, improved results can be obtained by giving plants a more accurately controlled diet, suited to their particular needs.

274 *Is the food for young plants different from that of older plants?*

As in humans, they often require simpler, less rich and complex foods. Excess of any one sort may be harmful.

275 *What are the main plant food chemicals?*

Carbon and water, but carbon they get free from the atmosphere.

276 *What about those plant foods absorbed from the soil?*

Nitrogen, potassium and phosphorus are far and away the most important. These are vital and constitute most fertilisers, but it is still important to realise that most of a plant's weight is derived from air and water and not from the soil.

277 *What is the effect of nitrogen?*

Broadly speaking, nitrogen helps in the growth of leaves and is very important where these are part of the food produced, as in the lettuce. Too little nitrogen would produce very pale green leaves and thin sickly growth.

278 *Supposing there is too much nitrogen. Does this show in any way?*

Yes, as rampant, soft growth, often dark green.

279 *How is potassium important?*

Potassium is usually referred to as potash and is concerned with the plant's change of sunlight into energy for the production of food in its leaves. It is particularly important too in the formation of fruit and, where this is the main part of the plant, potassium supplies must be carefully watched.

280 *What effects will shortage of potash have?*

Shortage will show itself largely by poor production of fruit. There are many complicated side effects, though, and much will depend upon how much nitrogen is also available. Nitrogen and potassium in effect balance each other inside the plant.

281 *What about excess potash? Will this give more fruit?*

Within limits, though real excess will produce tough, dark-coloured leaves and stems.

282 *What is the main function of phosphorus?*

It helps in many ways in maintaining health, especially in the growth of roots. That is why phosphorus-containing chemicals such as bone-meal are applied before sowing or transplanting, to encourage the development of good roots. Phosphorus deficiency is not easy to detect, though if the plants appear at all blue this may be a sign.

283 *I have been told that magnesium is also important for plants.*

Yes, though shortage is less common, because it is available in most soils and is often provided in chemicals given for other purposes. Tomatoes, however, need a lot of magnesium.

284 *Is shortage of magnesium visible?*

If the leaves between the veins turn pale then this may be an indication. A change of colour to a goldish bronze would be a further sign of magnesium shortage.

285 *Is iron in the soil very important to plants?*

Yes. It is vital, like vitamins for humans.

286 *How is iron given?*

Most soils and composts already contain enough iron. Shortage is only common on alkaline (chalky or limy) soils, though pot plants occasionally suffer in worn-out composts.

287 *How can I recognise deficiency of iron?*

If plant leaves turn pale yellow (or even white) then iron deficiency is the most likely cause.

288 *Can I bring on such a problem if I gave too much lime?*

Yes, in certain circumstances, though it would have to be a considerable excess to have this effect.

289 *Do plants differ in their need for iron?*

Some pot plants such as hydrangeas have difficulty in extracting soil iron and may therefore need special additional supplies, but fortunately most food plants do not present such problems.

290 *Are there other such chemicals which are only needed in small quantities?*

Several. These 'trace elements' include molybdenum, manganese, boron, sodium, etc.

291 *In what circumstances might one find a shortage of, for example, manganese?*

This sometimes arises when growing tomatoes if the soil is allowed to become very acid.

292 *What can make a soil acid?*

Shortage of lime might be a cause, but usually it starts with poor steam-sterilisation of the soil.

293 *How can I recognise manganese deficiency?*

It is not always very clear, the commonest symptons being that the plant is very easily broken and the leaves have a blue tinge.

55

294 *What about sulphur? Is this likely to be short?*

Sulphur is important to most plants but is rarely short as it forms part of many fertilisers.

295 *Are there any other chemicals where deficiency might be important?*

Only boron, a shortage of which can cause sickness in tomatoes but this is a rare matter and requires specialist advice.

296 *Is it possible to overfeed a plant?*

Yes, especially in greenhouses where the plant has only a limited amount of soil to grow in. Overfeeding with fertilisers can be as bad as under-feeding!

297 *How do I buy fertilisers? None in the shops seem to be called 'potassium', 'phosphorus' and so on?*

All fertilisers are mixtures or compounds under different names. Organic sorts are bone-meal, and hoof and horn meal, both good for phosphates. Dried blood contains nitrogen. Raw chemicals might be sulphate of ammonia, for nitrogen, and various sorts of potash, containing potassium.

298 *How do I know which to choose for a particular crop?*

Look under the plant name in the second part of this book, for any particular needs (see below for tomatoes). In general though, specially prepared mixtures of chemicals, commercially prepared for amateur greenhouses, are best for newcomers. They give balanced proportions, suited to most soils.

299 *Tomato fertilisers seem to be sold in several different types.*

The main sort is base fertiliser, usually a powder.

300 *Can I make this up at home?*

Yes. One formula, John Innes, is 2 parts hoof and horn meal, 2 parts superphosphate and 1 part sulphate of potash. (This gives a bit more potash than usual, but is very good.)

301 *What other fertilisers are used for tomatoes?*

Liquid feeds, which are standard, high potash and high nitrogen, used, broadly speaking, early, middle and late-season.

302 *What is a suitable standard liquid feed?*

6oz ammonium nitrate and 24oz potassium nitrate in 1 gal of warm water. Dilute 2oz of this solution in 2 gal of water before use (weekly).

303 *How is the high potash made?*

As above, but leave out the ammonium nitrate.

304 *And the high nitrogen solution?*

As the standard, but with 20oz ammonium nitrate instead of 6oz.

305 *Most manures seem to be powders or pellets. Are liquid manures different?*

Often these are the usual chemicals, but dissolved in water. (Again, you can buy them ready prepared, which is best at first.) They replace the traditional liquid manures made from animal dung, soot, etc.

306 *I like the traditional methods of doing things. How are the old type liquid manures prepared?*

Stable or farm manure must be well rotted by being stacked outdoors for six to eight weeks and turned occasionally. After this put some into a hessian sack and lower it into a tub full of water for a week. This makes a stock liquid which can be diluted just before use, to a very pale yellow.

307 *How much liquid manure shall I get from this?*

Roughly speaking, a sack of manure in an old fashioned barrel 3ft high gave 3 or even 4 fillings of water before being exhausted.

308 *Can poultry manure be used instead of farmyard manure?*

Yes, any sort of animal droppings will serve.

309 *How is soot manure made?*

By placing a bag full of soot in a tub of water for about a fortnight.

310 *How can I tell how strong such manures are?*

You cannot be certain. This is one of the difficulties of natural manuring. Old timers used the colour as a guide, aiming usually for a straw yellow. However, it is unlikely to be so strong as to injure your plants so it can do nothing but good in the vast majority of cases.

311 *I have heard that releasing carbon dioxide into a greenhouse can improve plant growth. Is this true?*

Yes. Providing the plants are growing vigorously and have ample warmth and light.

312 *How much extra carbon dioxide is usually needed?*

Less than 1,000 parts per million of air, which means roughly half a cubic foot for a greenhouse 10ft by 8ft.

313 *Does it matter much if you give more?*

It is better to give rather too little than too much.

314 *Can amateurs give carbon dioxide?*

It is possible but commercial equipment is extremely expensive. Some firms do have small apparatus though, and it may become cheaper if demand rises.

315 *How is this gas release arranged?*

Carbon dioxide is produced when you burn paraffin or propane gas in special burners. Another method is to use carbon dioxide compressed in cylinders or deep frozen to what is known as 'dry ice'.

316 *All these methods sound complicated. Is there no simpler way?*

Yes, fortunately. The straw-bale method of growing tomatoes (see questions 407–34) actually produces a significant amount of carbon dioxide as the straw rots. It is very good for tomatoes.

Compost Making

317 *Soils for seed-boxes and pots are*

called compost. *Is this the same as the rotted down garden rubbish we use outdoors?*

When outdoor gardeners refer to compost they mean rotted down remains of weeds, etc, made in a compost heap. The result is a very fertile, crumbly soil. For the greenhouse man, compost means a mixture of soil, chemicals, sand and peat in carefully chosen proportions.

318 *So it is really like making up your own ideal soil?*

Yes. You can adjust the proportions of the sand, peat and so on to provide a wide range of texture and add various chemicals.

319 *What are the main materials used in greenhouse composts?*

Soil, peat and sand are the usual main ingredients.

320 *What are soilless composts?*

These are made with vermiculite, perlite, raw peat or similar totally inert materials, used instead of soil.

321 *What is the advantage of this?*

Soils contain impurities, varying amounts of chemicals, and perhaps disease. Inert materials are clean and sterile.

322 *What proportions of sand, soil, peat, etc, are used?*

This depends upon the type of plants to be grown. One compost might have half soil, a quarter peat and a quarter sand for seedlings, the proportion of soil being increased for more mature plants.

323 *What about composts not containing soil?*

One type of this is made of half peat moss and half fine sand. Others use vermiculite and peat in about the same proportions.

324 *Do all these different composts contain enough plant food?*

No. The idea is that after you have mixed this basic 'bulk' material you add chemicals. For example, the famous John Innes compost has added lime, phosphates, etc in carefully controlled amounts.

325 *Is it possible to mix such composts at home?*

Yes. This saves money, but take great care with mixing and getting the proportions correct. John Innes compost for seeds is made by mixing 2 parts of soil (preferably sterilised), 1 part of peat and 1 part of coarse sand. Turn and mix this well together and keep it stored. Just before use add $\frac{1}{2}$oz of ground limestone and 1$\frac{1}{2}$oz of superphosphate to every bushel.

326 *Are the measurements by weight or bulk?*

All compost amounts are given by bulk for the major items (soil, peat and sand) and by weight per bushel for chemicals.

327 *What exactly is a bushel?*

This is a volume of soil which would fill a box 12in deep, 22in long and 10in wide.

328 *Why cannot the chemicals be added in bulk instead of being put in later?*

They start to 'work' in the compost soil and if left for any long time in store, would have given off part of their goodness, reducing the amount of plant food available.

329 *What crops would this compost suit best?*

This particular mixture was developed by John Innes Institution specially for growing seeds.

330 *What mixtures are there for more mature plants?*

Potting compost is a mixture of 7 parts of soil 3 parts of peat and 2 parts of coarse sand. You can add chemicals to this to give various strengths suited to more and more mature plants. They are then known as No 1, No 2 and No 3 composts.

331 *What chemicals do I add to make the No 1?*

To each bushel add $\frac{3}{4}$oz of ground limestone and $\frac{1}{4}$lb of John Innes base fertiliser (which you can buy ready-mixed).

332 *What does this base fertiliser contain?*

2 parts of hoof and horn meal, 2 parts superphosphate and 1 part sulphate of potash.

333 *Can I make up this base fertiliser myself?*

Yes, just follow the recipe above. Keep strictly to the proportions though. More or less of any chemical may upset the balance and will lessen the compost's value.

334 *How is the No 2 compost mixed?*

In the same way, but adding $\frac{1}{2}$lb instead of $\frac{1}{4}$lb of base fertiliser. The No 3 compost is the richest. Use $\frac{3}{4}$lb of base fertiliser per bushel.

335 *Why do you have to have so many kinds? Surely we could start off the seedlings direct in rich compost. It can hardly harm them!*

This would be a mistake. Strong chemicals can definitely injure very young plants. There are simply too many chemicals in the soil for the plant to be able to suck them out. It is far better for the young plants to be in too weak a compost than too strong.

336 *But what happens if they become starved?*

You can always add fertiliser, preferably in liquid form, as soon as seedlings start to grow, or better still, space them further apart in a fresh box of rather richer compost.

337 *Is the John Innes compost only used for seedlings?*

No, it is also one of the best materials to use in 'ring culture' of tomatoes and other crops.

338 *Which mixture is used for these?*

On the weaker side, with reduced sand, and no richer than No 2. You will find more detail about the different crops in later parts of the book.

339 *I have difficulty obtaining good, sterilised soil. Can I make up at home the soilless composts?*

Yes. Try a basic mixture of equal parts of peat moss and fine sand.

340 *What do I add to such a soilless compost?*

The simplest mix is 6–7oz of ground limestone and 8–10oz of a good general mixed fertiliser such as you can buy at most garden suppliers.

341 *Could you give more precise details of the chemicals needed?*

The number of mixtures possible is almost infinite and gardeners have different opinions upon their effectiveness. One which is widely accepted is to add to each bushel of compost $\frac{1}{4}$oz of ammonium nitrate, 2oz of superphosphate, 1oz of sulphate of potash, 4oz of ground limestone, 2oz of magnesium limestone and $\frac{1}{4}$oz of what is known as 'fritted trace elements'.

342 *What are these last? They sound odd!*

These are specially prepared chemicals of a kind only needed in tiny quantities by the plant. The 'fritted' part of the name refers to a special way they are prepared to enable plants to extract the chemicals more easily.

343 *Is the compost stored ready-mixed?*

Yes, so far, but just before use add 4oz of hoof and horn meal.

344 *Which are the best for amateur use, soil-containing or soilless composts?*

Always start by using soil compounds, since plants grown in soilless composts require more skilful attention with feeding, especially in the early stages.

345 *How is compost actually mixed?*

You need a fairly large, flat, smooth area such as a concrete garage floor or a very large, flat board. Make sure that it is dry. Always mix compost under cover if you can.

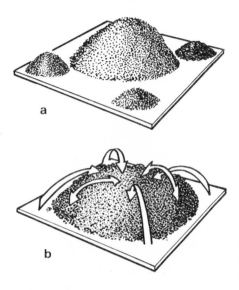

a

b

346 *Which of the ingredients are mixed first?*

The bulkiest ones. Start by placing the largest volume (which, in the case of John Innes, is the sterilised soil) in a heap. Then pile on top the other main ingredients, usually sand and peat. Turn the whole lot several times to make sure of an even mixing before adding chemicals.

347 *Since the amount of chemicals is proportionally so small, how can I best mix these in evenly?*

A good mixing method is to shovel the whole mass to one side and back again four times. This will give an almost perfect mix.

348 *Where should I store compost?*

Indoors, possibly in the greenhouse itself and certainly bring it into a warm place a week before use. It can then rise to the working temperature of the greenhouse. Cold composts may severely check the growth of young plants.

349 *I have no room indoors. Will outdoor storage do, if I make sure it is warmed well before use?*

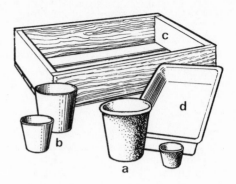

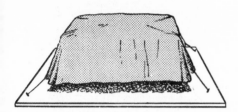

Make a smooth storage place, perhaps on loosely laid concrete slabs. Heap the compost and improvise some shelter with boards or plastic sheeting. This covering must be loose, so that air has access all round, but preventing rain from soaking the heap.

Cultivation Techniques: Seeding— Border Growing—Ring Culture— Straw Bale Culture

350 *For sowing seeds, what is the best type of container?*

Seed can be started successfully in almost anything that has a drainage hole, the old clay plant pots, modern plastic pots, wooden boxes, plastic trays—all are effective.

351 *What are the disadvantages of the traditional wooden boxes?*

They can rot and you have to wash and sterilise them (with formalin) before and after use or they may pass on disease.

352 *What are the advantages of plastic seed trays?*

They are easily kept clean and sterile simply by washing in warm water with a little detergent.

353 *Have they any disadvantages?*

Only the cost, and that you cannot easily make or repair them yourself, as is possible with wooden ones.

354 *How big are normal boxes?*

About 14in by 9in by 2in deep.

355 *Is it true that clay plant pots give better results than plastic?*

No. See the magnificent plants grown by our greatest nurseries, in plastic. For amateur work though, clay has some advantages. Plants in them may withstand neglect or errors better.

356 *How can the pot material make any difference?*

Clay is thick and water absorbent. It

retains a certain amount of moisture to tide a plant over any dry spell. It also retains heat better than plastic, so may give slight protection against varying warmth levels.

357 *What are the disadvantages of clay pots?*

They break, and must be washed and sterilised annually, for the porous clay can carry disease. Plastic needs washing too, but this is much easier.

358 *What about the use of peat or fibre pots? The makers claim a lot of advantages for them.*

Quite rightly too. They are excellent, especially for the larger type of seed such as tomatoes. Such big seeds can be planted singly and grown on in a tiny fibre pot. As the roots grow they push through the sides and the whole thing can be sunk into a bigger pot or direct into the border soil. The roots are never disturbed—a great help in getting speedy growth!

359 *Have they any disadvantages?*

Only their cost! A cheaper and effective alternative is to buy a soil block tool.

360 *What are soil blocks?*

Cubes of soil, compressed in a press

to retain their shape. Seeds are planted in small indentations in their tops. They work like fibre pots to some extent and are, of course, very cheap.

361 *How are seed trays and pots actually filled for seed sowing? Is it just a matter of filling the tray from a bag of compost?*

Not quite. Loose, stored compost will probably contain too much air and too little water (obviously this depends on the exact compost used).

362 *What is the method with a lightweight, soilless kind?*

Fill the tray up to its brim and draw it level with a straight-edged strip of wood. Then use a flat piece of board to press the compost firmly downwards $\frac{1}{4}$in below the edge of the tray. This will give adequate consolidation for most purposes.

363 *Are the composts with soil treated differently?*

They can be. Something depends upon whether you have managed to get a really free draining soil for your mixture, or whether it is rather heavy.

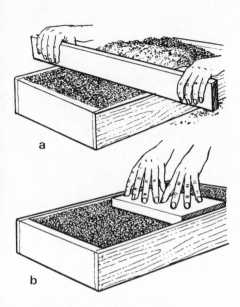

a

b

It is usually best to sieve the compost and then scatter about $\frac{1}{4}$–$\frac{1}{2}$in of the coarse sievings over the bottom of the pan before filling to the brim with the rest. This ensures there is adequate drainage at the bottom of the tray.

364 *Should this compost be pressed down too?*

A little. Bang the filled tray sharply on the bench to make it settle and press gently down over the surface with a flat, dry board.

365 *Should you ever put any other form of drainage in pots or trays?*

Not usually in trays, unless the compost is heavy. A clay pot will traditionally have a $\frac{1}{2}$in layer of broken pots or fine gravel in the bottom. Without this there is a tendency for them to become waterlogged. Plastic pots have less need because they have more holes, but again, heavy soil composts must have extra drainage.

366 *Presumably all compost must be watered before putting it into the heat trays?*

Not before filling. A wet compost will become a soggy mass if it is compressed whilst moist. Instead, fill the trays with dry compost, and water afterwards, preferably from underneath.

367 *How can you water from underneath?*

Lower the filled tray nearly to its brim in a trough of water (preferably lukewarm) until the top surface of the compost darkens. Then set the tray aside to drain thoroughly.

368 *Can't I water with a can? It would be much simpler.*

Only with great care. Top watering is often irregular, the surface becoming soaked and muddy. Use a very fine rose and give two or three sprinklings over an hour or so. Then let the box drain well before use.

369 *How are seeds actually sown?*

Fine seed must be sprinkled as delicately as possible over the surface and only lightly pressed in. It is not always necessary to cover such fine seed but if this is done, give only a light dressing of fine silver sand.

370 *Are bigger seeds treated differently?*

They need a heavier covering, buried under about $\frac{1}{8}$in of carefully sieved compost.

371 *Tomatoes have really big seeds. Are these sown individually?*

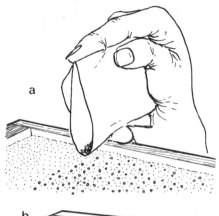

a

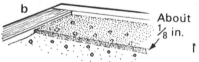

b

About
⅛ in.

This can be done. Place them in rows
to give about forty-eight small plants
evenly spaced on a normal sized tray.
An easy method is to scatter the seed
on a strip of glass, pushing them off
the edge one by one into position.
Cover them then with sieved compost
roughly ⅛in deep.

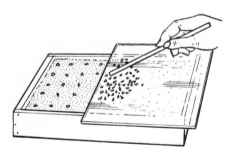

372 *What are pelleted seeds?*

These are seeds that have been given
a coating of chemical foods, designed
to assist the seed in the few days
after germination.

64

373 *Are they a great improvement on
plain seed?*

Outdoors, they can be much better.
Inside though, a good compost should
contain all that a seed needs, so the
extra cost is hardly worthwhile.

374 *How much light should newly
sown seed be given?*

a

b

c

None at all. Cover freshly sown seed
trays with sheets of glass to preserve
moisture and with newspaper to lower
the light level. Once the seeds have
germinated however—and this means
daily inspection—the paper must be
removed.

375 *When I do this, water accumulates
underneath the glass. Surely this
cannot be healthy?*

Every morning and evening, lift, turn
and wipe dry the glass.

376 *What temperature is required for seed germination?*

This varies with the type, but the vast majority of food seeds can be germinated between 55°F (12.8°C) and 60°F (15.6°C).

377 *Once the seedlings have germinated, scattered all over the tray, what is the next step?*

Pricking out, in which the seedlings are lifted and replanted into trays or pots.

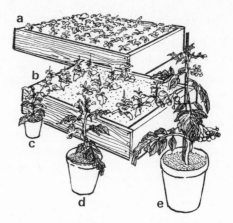

378 *At what stage is this best done?*

As soon as the seedlings are large enough to handle, which is usually when the first two leaves have appeared. The younger they are the better and the quicker they recover from the shock of transplanting.

379 *I would have thought that older seedlings would be stronger and better able to withstand moving about?*

This is a common mistake. Tiny seedlings are at their most active growth just as the second leaves open. The roots are pushing out vigorously. Later than this they will have established themselves to some extent and the newly grown roots will resent a sudden disturbance.

380 *Presumably the peat pot system comes into its own then?*

Yes, with individually sown seeds in fibre pots no transplanting is required.

381 *For greenhouse use, plants must be grown on into big pots. At what stage should seedlings be moved?*

Only in gradual stages. First from the seed tray to another tray, but with greater spacing. Then into small, medium and large pots as the plant grows.

382 *Why not shift the seedling direct into the biggest pot?*

Small seedlings' roots grow fastest near the edges of small pots. You can discover this by tipping out a vigorous plant. The roots will be most obviously growing near the pot sides. When they have fully developed, a shift to a slightly bigger pot keeps them growing out vigorously, till they are ready for 'hardening off', moving to the borders, into rings or to straw bales.

383 *What is the process known as 'hardening off'?*

This is accustoming seedlings, intended for outdoor use, to colder and windier conditions. They are usually moved from a greenhouse to a warm frame which is gradually ventilated more and more till the plants are ready for moving to open ground.

384 *When is this done?*

Timing varies with the kind of plant, but mostly we aim to have them hardened off as soon as the likelihood of frost is over.

385 *What preparation is needed when putting plants into borders?*

Apart from cultivating the soil, try to warm it up. Water it well a day or two beforehand (NOT an hour before!) Many gardeners plant on low mounds made above the border level.

386 *How is planting actually done?*

Gently! Nonetheless, make sure the roots are firmly held. Put in any supporting stakes or strings beforehand. Scoop out holes large enough to hold the whole root ball and take as much soil as possible with the plant from its pot.

387 *Do I water plants afterwards?*

Not if the soil is properly moist. Keep the house 'close' with vents shut for a day or two after, till the seedlings get

over transplanting shock.

388 *What is the technique known as 'ring culture'?*

'Rings' are 9in diameter circles of strong bitumen material, about 6in deep stood on a bed of ashes and filled with compost.

389 *So they are really like bottomless pots?*

Yes. Plants grown in rings have easy access to the ash beneath so that their roots can penetrate it freely, seeking water.

390 *What are the advantages of this system?*

Because such small quantities are needed, you can use first class sterilised soil and composts. Soil carried disease is reduced. The plants can accept much stronger feeding.

391 *Do not the rings actually restrict root growth?*

To some extent. The roots penetrating into the ash are largely used for extracting water and to hold the plant in place. The feeding roots are mainly confined within the ring itself.

392 *Surely this is a disadvantage? The plants could get more food in a bigger amount of soil. What really happens?*

The plant produces two types of roots, water absorbers spread widely in the ash and food absorbers in the rings. These last can absorb stronger chemicals than normal, and the plant itself can absorb them because the water collecting roots are so efficient.

393 *Does ring culture have any other advantages?*

Such small volumes of soil are easily heated, which makes it possible to put plants in them earlier.

394 *There must be disadvantages to the ring system or they would be used everywhere. What are these?*

With such a specialised system nothing else can be grown in the border soil. For example, you cannot plant anything between tomato plants whilst they develop.

395 *Presumably watering and feeding also take a lot of time?*

This is not such a problem as you might think, provided you have a hose to flood the ash bed regularly. Feeding, too, is often quickly done by liquids.

396 *Do you never put fertilisers on the ash?*

Never. Feeding is given either into the compost in the ring or by spraying over the leaves.

397 *In such small amounts of soil it must be easy to overdo the fertilising.*

This is one of the problems. You have to be on the sparing side with any feeding that you do, though the difficulty is not really great.

398 *Is it essential to use rings or could you not similarly use ordinary large plant pots or boxes?*

No. The main benefit with rings is the large mass of water-collecting roots that develop in the ash bed. This cannot happen with solid-based containers.

399 *Though you refer to ashes being used for the bed, presumably any well drained material such as gravel or sand, will do as well?*

No. Most gravel is far too coarse and rapid draining. The ideal material is fine household or boiler ash, well weathered.

400 *What does 'weathered' mean exactly?*

Exposed to the rain and wind for several months. The process washes away harmful chemicals such as sulphur, which would harm the plants.

401 *If I make an ash heap, how can I tell when weathering is complete?*

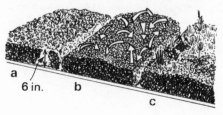

a

6 in.   b

c

Make the ash heap only shallow, up to 6in high and well spread out. Turn the heap each fortnight for six weeks. Then leave it until weeds and seedling grasses start to grow over it. This indicates that the poisons are disappearing. A month or so later the ash should be ready.

402 What would happen if I made a mistake and used ash that was not completely weathered?

The leaves of the plants develop a typical 'scorched' appearance on their edges.

403 Can anything be done then?

Heavy flooding of the ash, repeated twice a day for a week, may wash out the poisons. This is good practice in any case, the moment you lay out a new bed, or add to an established one.

404 How much ash is needed?

6in deep is customary, though slightly less is acceptable, especially over light, or medium soils.

405 What other material might be used instead of ash?

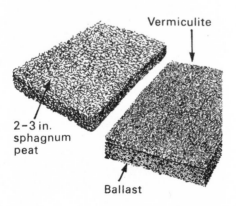

Vermiculite

2-3 in. sphagnum peat

Ballast

A 2–3in bed of sphagnum peat is the next best. It retains water well, is sterile and carries no disease. It must, though, be replaced each season. The builders' material called ballast, a mixture of sand and gravel, will also serve, though not so efficiently as ash. A 1in deep layer of horticultural vermiculite over this, raked in, will help a lot.

406 I have some granulated vermiculite left over from my roof insulation. Can I use this?

No. This is often a different type from horticultural grades.

407 What is straw bale culture?

This is growing tomato plants in small quantities of soil placed on top of half (or quarter) straw bales, arranged in rows along the greenhouse.

408 This seems an extraordinary method. What is the basis of it?

The straw is caused to rot by applying chemicals. This heats up the bale.

The plants in their tiny heap of soil are separated from the border soil itself and so run much less risk of soil-borne disease.

409 *Presumably this early warmth is an advantage?*

Yes. You give a really good start to all your plants.

410 *Earlier you said that straw gave off carbon dioxide when it rots. Is this also an advantage of the method?*

Yes, though it is difficult to say to what extent. The precise control of the carbon dioxide is impossible.

411 *Are there any other advantages?*

Yes. It is easy to remove used-up bale remnants. They are quite light and will rot down for outdoor compost very readily. The straw is usually fairly cheap to buy since high quality is not required. It should not, however, already have started to rot and more especially should not be mouldy when bought.

412 *A system that gives you early warmth, protection from disease and vigorous growth must have some disadvantages too?*

Too vigorous growth may itself be a problem. The roots soon pass all through the bale and may even reach the underlying soil. Naturally, too, the bales are fairly bulky to handle.

413 *How small an amount of straw is the minimum?*

Probably a quarter of a bale, which can be about 2¼ sq ft and 8–10in high.

414 *Are these heavy?*

No, only about 10–12lb each.

415 *What are the watering and feeding problems?*

The bales are always thoroughly soaked when being placed in position. Afterwards you will have to water frequently since drainage is rapid and the warmth dries out the bales very quickly. Straw bales are not to be used if you have to leave the greenhouse entirely for days at a time.

416 *How are the straw bales arranged?*

It is usual to break the bales up into halves or even quarters and then arrange them in three lines down the greenhouse, one on either side and one down the centre. With small houses the centre row may be omitted.

417 *When is this done?*

About three weeks before you want to plant and as soon as the temperature is 50°F (10°C).

418 *What is the next step?*

Watering. Over a period of a week, thoroughly hose down the straw. It must be absolutely soaked right through, not just wet on the surface.

419 *When are chemicals applied to the straw?*

When soaking is complete. Start with ¾lb of nitro chalk to every bale, proportionately less for half or quarter bales. Scatter this over the top of the bale surface and sprinkle it with water. (On this occasion do not use too much water or you might wash the nitro chalk right through the bale.) After about another five days give another ½lb of nitro chalk.

420 *Is this the only chemical which is used?*

It is certainly one of the most important because a week later you put yet another 1½lb of nitro chalk on but this time accompanied by 9oz of nitrate of potash, 6oz of magnesium sulphate, and 3oz of sulphate of iron (some gardeners substitute super-phosphate for some of the nitro chalk).

421 *Presumably the bales have started rotting after all this?*

Yes. The soaking wet conditions, together with the nitrogen food provided by the chemicals, will encourage the rotting bacteria to get to work very powerfully indeed. The straw bales rapidly heat up to about 130°F (54.4°C) in the middle and you will have to keep them constantly watered.

422 *How can I check the bale temperature?*

As we said earlier, a soil thermometer is a good investment for a gardener growing food in a greenhouse. You can thrust these deep down into the bales or soil and get an accurate reading.

423 *When is the actual growing compost put in place?*

Wait for the temperature in the bales to fall to 100°F (37.8°C) Then they are ready for planting.

424 *How is the compost or soil arranged?*

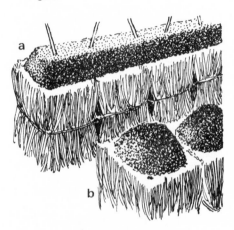

Use John Innes No 2 or equivalent compost just as for ring culture. Simply arrange it in 6in deep strips right along the straw bales. Alternatively, make heaps 6in or 8in high at each plant position.

425 *Are the plants then put at once into the compost?*

Not immediately. Always wait for at least one to two days to let the compost rise in temperature. Remember that with tomatoes, continuous growth without checks is vital for success. Planting in cold compost is always a mistake.

426 *What is the spacing for bale grown plants?*

Much closer than for the other methods, 1ft apart even is not too little in many cases. Of course, you have to watch the shading question, especially on the south side of east–west greenhouses.

427 *Must the plants be central in the bale?*

No, they can be towards the edges because the root systems will develop inwards in any case, seeking the richest source of food.

428 *Is watering needed immediately after planting?*

Yes, and regularly afterwards, otherwise the compost will dry out and the plants will die. As much as 2gal per day per bale may be needed!

429 *How are the plants supported—by*

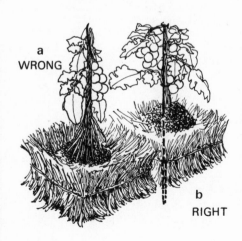

a
WRONG

b
RIGHT

string in the usual way, looped round the stem?

No. Never do this because the tops of the bales will sink as they rot. If your supporting string is actually tied to the plant it may pull it right out! It is better to tie the plants to strings or wires attached to pegs driven into the border soil beneath the bales.

430 *It seems to me that the stems will be very crowded at only 1ft apart. Are they always trained directly upwards?*

No. It is a good practice to spread the growing stems as far apart as possible, drawing them out into 'v' patterns. This gives the upper leaves space to develop.

431 *How does feeding of straw bale plants differ from other methods?*

The rotting straw provides most of the nitrogen so you only have to provide potash (often as nitrate of potash), though often for much more of the season than with the other methods.

432 *Is this given as liquid or powder?*

Either will serve, though drainage is very rapid through straw especially, so powder may be fractionally better. Apply it to the compost, not to the straw bale but keep it away from the stem of the plant.

433 *Straw bales seem to involve a lot of work. Is this really worthwhile?*

If tomato diseases are a problem in your district, you will find straw bales give a marked improvement, whilst cucumbers enjoy the rich feeding possible.

434 *The greatest trouble with straw*

*bales seems to me to be watering.
Is there any way I can reduce the
frequency with which this is needed?*

Lining the greenhouse with polythene
will maintain a much more humid
atmosphere, and cut down water
needs. However, there is really no
substitute for a twice daily soaking.

Greenhouse Hygiene, Pests and Diseases

435 *Do greenhouse plants suffer much
from pests and disease?*

This greatly depends on the skill with
which they are cultivated. The most
important fault is to give too little
ventilation. A hot and muggy
greenhouse atmosphere suits very few
plants.

436 *Is there a regular routine of
spraying that will ensure pest-free
crops?*

No. There are, it is true, many
powerful chemicals which will deal
with an outbreak of pests (and certain
diseases). Unfortunately, though,
pests soon develop resistance to
these sprays if you use them regularly,
year in, year out.

437 *How can using a pest killer help
the pests?*

In any large number of a particular
pest there will always be a few
individuals who are more resistant to
a spray than others. These individuals
will survive and their offspring will
probably inherit the same resistance.
The next generation will therefore
have a larger proportion of resistant
individuals which again will tend to
survive. The result is the build-up of a

type which cannot be killed by this
particular spray. This has happened
to a number of pesticides in the past
and no doubt will do so in the future.

438 *Some insecticides I have tried
were once very effective but now seem
less so. Is this due to the build-up of
resistance?*

Quite possibly. It is always best to
use a variety of different materials
throughout the season. On the shelves
of nurserymen and gardener suppliers
are various types of spray. By having
several sorts in use you help prevent
the build-up of resistance.

439 *What then can I do to keep down
the pest risk?*

In winter, thoroughly wash down the
greenhouse and everything in it with
powerful disinfectant.

440 *Why should this be done in the
winter: pests are surely more active
in the summer?*

Yes, but they all have to survive over
the winter and it is then easier to kill
them. They often over-winter as tiny
eggs or chrysalids. In winter, too, the
greenhouse is usually much emptier.
You can get into every nook and
cranny with the disinfectant. You can
also sterilise all your pots and boxes.
This will give you a flying start in the
spring and you are very much less
likely to be bothered by pests in the
following season.

441 *Does the same apply to disease?*

It helps, though most diseases are
caused by viruses or fungi. Virus
diseases are often transmitted in the
the plants themselves and buying
healthy stock is one good defence.

(You can buy some plants certified free of virus.) Fungus diseases are nearly always helped along by too moist conditions in the greenhouse and in particular by irregularity of watering and ventilation.

442 *You stress regularity—why is this?*

Any plant needs regular food, air, warmth and water in the correct proportions for the time of day and the season. Its use of these vital elements is closely interrelated. Too much of any factor—water, heat, chemicals—can upset this balance. It may only be for a few hours, but it takes toll of the plant's health.

443 *So, after winter sterilisation, a regular routine also helps to give healthy plants?*

Yes. Establish a pattern, then stick to it. Many diseases of greenhouse plants are simply the result of irregular watering or opening of the vents, neglect of the heating system and so on. The temperature may rise sky high one hot day with the vents left shut and then drop next day when they are left open far into the night. Greenhouse work calls for regular attention to routine detail.

444 *How do I know what chemicals to buy for the control of pests and diseases if these do appear?*

Some indication is given in the alphabetic section of this book later. New chemicals appear from time to time and many of these are excellent. However, there is one point to stress. Always use the chemicals which are listed in the Agricultural Chemicals Approval Scheme. These have been tested to be safe for food growing.

445 *I have used insecticides from time to time but they always seem to be very weak. Can I help their effort (even at more expense) by putting them on stronger?*

Never alter the proportions either of insecticides, disease-control sprays or indeed fertilisers from the manufacturers' recommendations. Many of these have no damaging effect on the plants then, but could do them injury used at, say, treble the dose.

446 *Can this ever make the food poisonous to eat?*

Not to a really dangerous extent, but it can give a taint. Many sorts should not be sprayed directly on to fruit which is about to be harvested, but this is common sense anyway.

447 *What is greenhouse fumigation?*

Filling the greenhouse with poisonous vapour or gas to kill off insect pests and some diseases.

448 *What methods are used?*

For amateur work, smoke-bombs are burned, after sealing up all cracks in the structure, to trap the fumes.

449 *What chemicals are used in fumigation?*

Traditionally napthaline, nicotine, sulphur, etc, but there are many modern recipes now available, under different trade names. It is vital to follow the manufacturers' instructions exactly.

450 *Must all plants be removed before fumigation take place?*

Not as a rule, unless sulphur

73

fumigants are being used against fungus attack.

Choosing your Seeds and Plants

451 *There are dozens of named varieties of food plants. How can I possibly choose the best?*

Ideally, see your local nurseryman or garden centre (preferably a practical grower) and discuss your precise needs. Tell him the size of your greenhouse, its kind and power of heating and the mixture of crops you are attempting.

452 *Why are there so many varieties of plants?*

Growers have many differing needs. Varieties may be large or small, some enormous for large greenhouses, others very short for growth in frames. Some give heavy crops. Others have fruit of especially delicate flavour, or produce fruit of regular size, good for canning. Resistance to disease, too, is a very important factor.

453 *In seedsmen's catalogues some plants are marked 'F1'. What does this mean?*

These are hybrid plants produced by crossing two varieties. The cross is freshly made each year. For technical reasons this gives better results than sowing the seeds of the hybrid plants themselves.

454 *I have no nurseryman to ask. Are there no general rules about selection of variety that will help?*

You can work systematically in this way. First, consider the season at which the plant will be growing: do you want very early, mid season or late crops? (Frost resistance may be important for cold greenhouse or frame work.) Secondly, how big a plant do you need—very large growing, moderate, or small for under cloches? Thirdly, are you after the maximum possible size and quality of individual fruits or would you prefer a larger crop of smaller fruits? Fourthly, have you reason to believe that your land or greenhouse is carrying any virus or other disease? Looking through a good seedman's catalogue you should be able to draw up a short list of varieties with the necessary qualities of season, size, cropping habit and disease resistance.

455 *I have heard that grafted tomato plants are occasionally used where soil disease is present. What exactly is grafting?*

Closely related plants will often grow together if their cut surfaces are held firmly touching for a few days. This makes it possible to join the disease resistant roots of one plant to the stem of another.

456 *Why should this be desirable?*

Disease resistant tomato varieties often produce poorer crops than those that are not resistant. By grafting the roots of the first on to the stems of the second you can get good croppers with resistant roots.

457 *How is this grafting done?*

The two plants are placed side by side and the stems of both drawn together. Where they touch, the skin is cut out. They are held firmly to each other with adhesive tape until the stems unite. After this the leafy top of the root resistant kind is cut away.

74

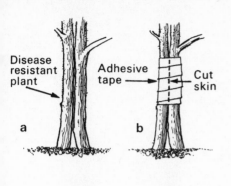

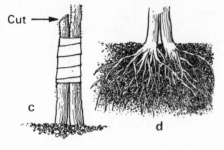

458 *So the grafted plant ends up with two completely separate sets of roots?*

Yes. Both roots are usually preserved and the result is a vigorous plant resistant to many kinds of fungus disease but with stems and leaves that produce good crops.

459 *Are grafted plants also immune to the potato root eel worm which does so much damage to tomato crops?*

Unfortunately no.

460 *Can one buy ready-grafted plants?*

Yes. Some nurserymen supply them but they may cost nearly as much again as ordinary plants.

Part 2
A–Z of Fruit and Vegetables

Apricots

461 *Where in the greenhouse should apricots be grown?*

In most amateur houses, as a fan against a wall (the back wall of a lean-to or the end wall of a span-roofed house).

462 *When are they planted?*

In late autumn or early winter.

463 *Can I plant a single tree or will I need another one to fertilise the fruit?*

All apricots are self-fertile so you only need one.

464 *What soil preparation is required?*

As with all permanent plants, deep digging—a yard depth of good soil is not too much. The future of the tree depends on having adequate soil to develop a vigorous root system.

465 *Do they need high temperatures?*

No, they will even set crops outdoors, in frost-free areas. The cool house will serve.

466 *My site is rather wet. Should I put in artificial drainage?*

Good drainage is vital. Fill the bottom 6in of the planting pit with brick rubble, broken stones and coarse sand and gravel.

467 *Will any fertilisers be needed?*

Phosphates are helpful, given in the form of coarsely ground bone-meal but otherwise any normally fertile soil will serve. Too rich manuring may lead to rank growth with delayed or reduced fruiting.

468 *Will extra lime be required?*

Lime rubble dug in will help in all but calcareous soils.

469 *Will an apricot require pruning?*

Yes, the general methods being similar to peaches (see the questions under that heading). However there are some differences because apricots bear fruit on old and new wood, whereas peaches only bear on new wood.

470 *How is this allowed for?*

When developing the framework of a peach tree, all the old wood is cut out. With apricots only half the old wood is cut out. The rest is merely shortened.

77

471 *I have had an apricot for some time and suddenly several of its branches died. Is this some sort of disease?*

You probably had a very cold spell in the previous winter and the tree was struck by frost. However, dieback does occur sometimes in other circumstances. Its cause is obscure.

472 *Can I treat the tree at all?*

There is no actual cure, but if you prune off into good wood, you can train the remainder back into shape again, when it will often be quite healthy.

473 *What other diseases attack the apricot?*

Those which are common to peaches and which are described in that section (see questions 828–30).

474 *How much fruit can I expect to get from a single tree?*

This is almost impossible to say. It depends on too many factors—the variety, age, temperature at setting time, skill in pruning and just plain luck! In a good year, though, you might get a fruit on every 6in of stem —quite a lot on a mature tree!

Asparagus

475 *Can asparagus be forced in greenhouses?*

If you have a good outdoor bed of well grown plants, this is possible.

476 *What is the actual treatment?*

Similar to seakale (see question 861)

78

and other vegetables. In November, select good strong plants, lift and plant them in boxes 3in deep in fine, damp soil or peat.

477 *Are they kept dark?*

Yes. It is common to put them under the greenhouse benching and fairly rapid development of shoots will take place.

478 *When are they ready for cutting?*

Through midwinter, cutting the shoots before they are more than 6–8in high.

479 *What temperature will be required?*

Aim at 65°F (18.3°C) for a rapid growth, though lower will serve, giving later results.

480 *When can the plants be returned to the outdoor bed?*

It is best not to do so. Forced plants are weakened and are better thrown away. Divide remaining plants to give more forcing stock for the succeeding season.

Aubergine

481 *Can you grow aubergines in a greenhouse?*

Yes, though we have not done this ourselves. The seed is put into boxes in a warm house in February and the seedlings potted on gradually up into pots 7–10in across.

482 *What type of compost will they need?*

Aubergines are rich feeders and like

a good quality compost such as John Innes No 2 or No 3.

483 *Do they like a moist or an airy atmosphere?*

They respond well to plenty of ventilation at all times. Indeed, you can grow these plants outside in the latter part of their lives, putting them out after all risk of frost has vanished.

484 *At what stage should they be picked?*

As individual fruits become ripe, remove them, as this encourages more to develop.

Capsicums

485 *Is a greenhouse helpful when growing peppers (capsicums)?*

Yes, though we have never grown them ourselves. Friends tell us that peppers need a long season to ripen properly, so starting them under glass in February or March is a great help.

486 *What sort of compost or soil is best?*

Light but rich. Use manures or well rotted garden refuse dug in before-hand.

487 *What about lime?*

Do not overdo this. A pH of about 6.0 will do nicely.

488 *I have been told that peppers need lots of water.*

Yes, though this does not mean they like waterlogged ground! Overhead summer spraying will do good and plants in pots or trays must never dry out.

489 *When exactly is seed sowing done?*

In a warm house sow first in February. In frames, a little later, up to April.

490 *When are they transplanted?*

As soon as the seedlings can be handled. For fine plants, shift these to 3in pots, then later to 6in pots to mature.

491 *Can I transplant them outdoors?*

Yes, after a gradual hardening off. Space the plants about 18in apart in a warm, sunny border in June.

492 *What fertilisers are needed?*

Apart from the compost and manure dug in earlier, superphosphate is commonly used to stimulate growth. If leaves turn yellow with nitrogen deficiency, apply 1oz per square yard of ammonium sulphate.

493 *Should I keep a special plot for peppers?*

No. Change their position each year.

494 *What pests are troublesome to peppers?*

Mostly red spider and begonia mite. Brisk spraying with plain water helps control these, or you can use a sulphur fumigant under glass.

495 *When will the peppers be ready to harvest?*

About August/September. Use them as soon as possible after picking. Any not wanted immediately are best left on the plants as they do not store well.

Celery

496 *When are plants of celery first seeded in the greenhouse?*

For very early crops in February in a warm house. Follow on with more seedlings in a cooler house in March/April.

497 *How big will they be at this time?*

Aim to have them 4in tall at least.

498 *What temperature is needed?*

An even 60°F (15.6°C), until they are ½in high and ready to be transplanted further apart.

499 *What compost is best for them?*

John Innes (seed), though many gardeners use 50/50 fine soil and leaf mould.

500 *Will they take up much space?*

Celery plants are very tiny and slow growing so only a box or two will be needed. Once they start to grow you can put them out into a warmish frame to develop further.

501 *How far apart should they be spaced?*

Only 2–3in each way.

502 *When are they moved from the frame?*

When the soil warms up in April/May.

Chicory

503 *Can you suggest a salad crop that will be ready in winter?*

Try chicory. You can grow this outdoors in summer, and then force roots for winter use.

504 *Can I use my cool greenhouse to force chicory?*

Yes. Indeed, you need not use a greenhouse at all. A warm dark shed or even the cupboard under the stairs will do!

505 *When are the seeds put in?*

Outdoors in late spring in rows about 15in apart.

506 *Are they thinned out to any degree?*

Yes, the final spacing should be 9in and the plants simply kept hoed as their deep tap roots develop.

507 *When is forcing started?*

In autumn. Dig up the plants and place them in moist soil in deep boxes. Put them under the greenhouse staging and cover them with black polythene.

508 *Will they require any further attention during this period?*

Apart from making sure the soil does not dry out, none. As the leaves appear they will be pale and blanched. Make sure that the dark covering allows enough space for these leaves' free development.

Corn—Sweet Corn

509 *Is sweet corn a suitable greenhouse crop?*

Corn is hardy enough to grow outside, but early crops benefit if started under glass. It is a valuable but often neglected crop.

510 *When are seeds sown?*

Under glass, in April. Later, in warm areas, you can sow outdoors.

511 *Do the seedlings grow rapidly?*

If sown in small peat pots or boxes and kept only moderately warm they will be ready for hardening off by May or early June. Growth then continues to be rapid, in good soil.

512 *When will the cobs be ready?*

From mid-July (with luck) through August and early September.

Cucumbers

513 *How difficult are cucumbers to grow?*

They are probably the easiest of all greenhouse crops. The only problem is that they like hot and moist conditions and this may not be easy to provide, if your greenhouse has other plants in it at the same time.

514 *So it may be difficult to grow a few plants in a greenhouse with tomatoes?*

It is far better if you can divide the greenhouse into two sections, one part kept hotter and more humid than the other.

515 *Will a temporary partition of polythene sheet be enough?*

Yes, though not ideal. Hang two thicknesses overlapping and spaced 2in apart, like double curtains.

516 *Will I have no success if I grow a cucumber in with tomatoes?*

Provided you give it just that little extra attention, a little bit more water spraying, etc, and keep it as warm as possible, away from draughts, you should still get a crop.

517 *When are cucumbers sown?*

From February onwards, though keen growers aim at a succession and may seed through late winter and spring.

518 *Are seeds put directly into the border soil or into pots?*

Singly, in 3in pots full of John Innes No 1 or similar compost.

519 *Presumably they have to be kept warm?*

Yes. You need 65°F (18.3°C) minimum, preferably 75°F (23.9°C) by day, but then you will get plants within two days. If they haven't started growth vigorously on the third day, throw them away even if germination is by then taking place under the soil. You will probably only need one or two plants, so if you put six seeds in you can afford to select the most vigorous.

520 *When are they transplanted?*

Once they have grown to 6in tall, shift them into 5in pots. They may need a cane at this stage.

521 *In border growth, what is the best soil?*

One containing a large proportion of good, well rotted farmyard manure (though these days this is a little difficult to obtain).

522 *Is there a good alternative when we have just a single plant?*

In this case it is probably worth the cost of using John Innes No 2 compost. This is rich but not over-strong.

523 *What temperature is needed in the greenhouse before the plants are put out?*

60°F (15.6°C) at night is enough and up to 80°F (26.7°C) during the day.

524 *When growing more than one, how far apart should they be put?*

Not less than 2ft. They are vigorous growers.

525 *Presumably cucumbers are grown up strings or wires. They seem to grow so vigorously that training must be quite a job?*

You can grow them like tomatoes, allowing only a single stem to develop up a supporting string. This is a straightforward method and useful if you are not wanting the largest crop and haven't got a lot of space.

526 *Should I pinch out the side growths?*

Mostly, but save some right up the plant, pinching them back to four leaves.

527 *What is a better method for bigger crops?*

Allow more growth, tying several stems into horizontal wires. These stems should spread somewhat to allow the maturing fruit to hang down.

This is important because a growing cucumber that touches anything else will curl towards it. Perfectly free hanging is essential for straight, first-class fruit.

528 *Are the side shoots still pinched back?*

Yes, as for single stems, to four leaves.

529 *I have been told to remove the male flowers. Why is this?*

If these are allowed to stay, the fruits may be pollinated and become ill tasting, seedy or bitter.

530 *How do I know which are the male flowers?*

The two sorts of flowers do look very similar. The female, though, has a very tiny cucumber behind it.

531 *Are there cucumbers that do not produce male flowers?*

Yes. Quite a large number of varieties have only female flowers which do not produce bitter cucumbers.

532 *What is the best fertiliser for growing cucumbers?*

Provided they are getting adequate water, farmyard manure or even a dressing of rich garden soil, they need little additional feeding early on. If this isn't available a high nitrogen tomato fertiliser can be helpful.

533 *Are liquid manures then beneficial?*

Yes, twice a week whilst fruit is forming.

534 *Presumably, since cucumbers like moist conditions, you should not ventilate very much?*

This is quite wrong. Cucumbers need ventilation as much as any other crop or they will not be able to breathe properly. It is true, though, that this ventilation should ideally not reduce the humidity too much.

535 *How is this possible? Ventilation removes the moist air!*

You will have to spray constantly. Shading the greenhouse can help too.

536 *Can cucumbers be grown in rings like tomatoes?*

This is uncommon but possible. The compost used is usually a mixture of soil and farmyard manure rather than the John Innes type mixed composts.

537 *I have been told you can also grow cucumbers in pots and boxes?*

Yes. A 10in pot or the equivalent size of wooden box would be quite big enough to accommodate the root system of a cucumber, though you can't expect the vigorous growth that you get from border culture.

538 *Could I grow a cucumber indoors, in my house?*

Not very easily. They need a hot and humid atmosphere that you would find very uncomfortable! Moreover, a nightly drop to a low temperature, as is common in houses, would check

them badly.

539 *For an amateur with only a small greenhouse, what would be the best way of growing cucumbers?*

By knocking up an outdoor frame and heating it by digging in plenty of partly rotted farmyard manure. This heats the soil. You save greenhouse space and get quite good crops, though the cucumbers are not of as high quality as greenhouse grown sorts.

540 *When are frame plants put out?*

April/June. You only need one for each frame.

541 *How much water is needed?*

This depends on the weather. In cool periods keep the frame closed except for occasional half hour spells of ventilation to change the air. Water only to keep the soil moist. In warm weather spray twice a day at least and ventilate to prevent too high temperatures.

542 *To get the longest fruiting season, should I leave fruit to grow huge, or cut them small?*

Cut regularly. This encourages the plant to keep on expanding young fruit over a longer period.

543 *What cucumber disease causes the stem to go soft and brown at the base?*

Canker. An effective traditional treatment is to rub the part with a mix of 10 parts hydrated lime, 3 parts copper sulphate powder and 3 parts flowers of sulphur.

544 *My cucumber has produced pale*

83

*green spots, yellowing and growing
bigger. Can I cure this?*

No. Destroy the plant and next year
try a variety resistant to leaf spot
disease.

545 *What is mosaic disease?*

A virus that causes the leaves to
become mottled. Nothing can be done
for a severe attack. Burn the plant—
do not make it into compost.

546 *Do pests attack cucumbers?*

Not many. Red spider may be
troublesome, but spraying with
commercial preparations can control
them.

547 *I am growing my tomatoes by the
straw bale method (see questions
407–34). Can I grow cucumbers the
same way?*

Yes, cucumbers quite like the rich
feeding possible on straw bales.

Figs

548 *Can I grow figs in the
greenhouse?*

Yes. Indeed, you can grow them
outside, although conditions in a
greenhouse are somewhat more
favourable for fruiting.

549 *What type of house suits it best?*

Warm and sunny but not too humid.
The rear wall of a lean-to is quite
good. If you have a big lean-to you
might plant one fig in conjunction with
a fan grown peach.

550 *What soil preparation is needed?*

Soil should be preferably on the light
side and certainly not heavy clay.
Make sure there is plenty of lime
rubble and drainage material dug in
when preparing the planting site.
However, there are peculiarities in
planting a fig since a very restricted
root growth is desirable.

551 *How is excess development of the
roots prevented?*

A reliable old method is to dig out a
hole 1sq yd and 2ft deep and then
actually build a wall round it of old
bricks or concrete blocks. Cover the
bottom with rammed bricks and stone
rubble about 1ft thick and then fill up
with soil of the kind described earlier.

552 *This sounds a most unlikely thing
to benefit any plant!*

In its native Mediterranean the fig has
to cling to rocky terrain with limited
soil and does best in these conditions.
In rich soil it will tend to develop
bigger and bigger, but fruit very little.

553 *When are figs best planted?*

In spring, usually about April, though
if you buy them in pots it does not
really matter.

554 *How are figs best trained?*

As fans, spreading out the shoots and
attaching them to straining wires in a
similar way to peaches.

555 *What type of pruning is given?*

Practically none, except that after you
have gathered the crop you can
remove any shoots which appear to
be crowded or growing in an
undesirable direction.

556 *I believe that the figs have to be thinned in some way?*

Yes, figs fruit rather peculiarly, right up the length of the stem of the fruit shoot, the biggest at the base, naturally.

557 *Which of the fruits are removed?*

Study the shoot carefully. At the bottom will be a few fairly large figs which are obviously going to ripen to maturity. Above these will be some small fruits which will not develop in this country. These are taken off.

558 *At the tip of the fruit shoots on my fig there appear to be yet more fruits in a very early stage of development. Are these taken off too?*

No. These are next year's crop. You must leave them in place.

559 *So in effect we leave the largest (lowest) and the smallest (highest) and take off those in the middle?*

This is correct. You do need judgment though. Much depends on the heat in your house. You may be able to mature some of the 'in between' figs in a sunny area.

French Beans

560 *I am very fond of French beans. I wonder if these can be forced through winter in greenhouses?*

Certainly, there are climbing varieties that do best in the larger kinds of houses with height to allow full development.

561 *We have a lean-to on one wall of the house. Would this be suitable?*

French beans are excellent grown against a house wall where the maximum height is available.

562 *When are the seeds sown?*

During the winter, from September right through to March.

563 *Are they sown in pots or boxes?*

For the small number needed it is best to sow them singly in peat pots.

564 *When are they put out into position into borders?*

About three to five weeks later, spaced about 18in apart along the border.

565 *What soil preparation is needed?*

The normal border soil of a cultivated greenhouse is adequate for beans. A light dressing of a general fertiliser will do no harm, shortly before they are put in.

566 *What type of support is required?*

Canes, string or branches will do, exactly as out-of-doors.

567 *Will the growing plants need any pruning?*

You are liable to get over-lush growth with a warm greenhouse, so keep the plant in bounds by trimming back side growths.

568 *What water will be needed?*

The plants must never dry out completely. An early morning spray over the leaves as well will greatly help in sunny weather.

569 *Can beans be grown in pots*

instead of in the border?

Dwarf kinds can be grown in 8–10in pots (smaller sizes do not allow the development of a large enough root system).

570 *How many seeds are put into each pot?*

Five to six, spaced 2–3in apart, mostly round the edge of the pot.

571 *What potting compost is used?*

Try John Innes No 2, but only half fill the pots first. The aim is to develop a root system low down in the bottom of the pot.

572 *Is the pot filled up later?*

Yes. As the plants develop and grow above 6–8in tall, raise the level of compost gradually until the pot is full.

Fruit

573 *Can fruit trees be grown indoors in pots and tubs?*

Yes, and many types actually benefit by having a restricted root system. It seems to bring them on to early flowers and fruit. They are only brought inside part of the year, though, and do take up a lot of space. A big, old conservatory will serve well.

574 *What trees give best results?*

Apples, cherries, nectarines, peaches, pears and plums. Their culture is as outdoors, but earlier fruit setting is possible.

575 *Are standards or bush types usually grown?*

Bushes are much more easy to control. Small standards, well pruned, are sometimes seen.

576 *What type of compost is used?*

The best are those based on the traditional well-rotted turf (you can often get enough of this by trimming 1–2in off the edge of a lawn). Stack it upside down and cover the heap with a 2in layer of good soil. Rotting takes place over several months and the resulting compost is first-class.

577 *Will it need mixing with other materials?*

Farmyard manure stacked in the same way is ideal, mixed 2–3 parts rotted turf to 1 part of manure. Add 1 part of very coarse sand and turn the mixture well.

578 *Can I use chemicals instead of farmyard manure?*

Well rotted turf with a general mixed fertiliser is still an excellent soil but do add the sand. It improves drainage and soil texture considerably.

579 *How often should the soil be changed in tubs?*

Every second or third year. Lift the plant, shake and crumble away the soil and replant in fresh compost.

580 *How can tub plants be manured?*

Liquid fertilisers are easiest. Fine powders can be sprinkled on, but do not overdo either sort. Over-manuring can do great harm.

581 *Big tubs and plants are hard to replant. Can the soil be replaced from above?*

Yes, and some gardeners do so regularly, every year.

582 *How is fresh soil added to a full tub?*

Scrape away the top 2–3in of old soil by hand, not damaging the roots. Loosen and remove 1in of soil round the sides too, as deeply as possible. Then repack with moist (not soaking wet) compost.

583 *Are pot grown fruit kept in the glass-house all the year round?*

No. It is better to take them outdoors once you have harvested the fruit. The warm, fresh air of late summer will do them a world of good.

584 *Presumably they are brought in before the cold weather starts?*

No. In most parts of the country they are reasonably hardy and except in the severest winters actually benefit by standing outdoors until the first blooms appear. It is then that they are brought into the house for rapid blossoming and fruiting.

585 *What pruning will be required?*

Growth will usually be restricted by the pot but keep the plant open to the sun or ripening may be affected. Give each plant the type of pruning it normally gets outdoors, though the amount is not likely to be great.

Grapes

586 *Is it really possible for amateurs to grow good grapes?*

Yes, cultivation is relatively simple,

especially if you do not try for very early crops.

587 *Do I need a big greenhouse to grow grapes successfully?*

Grapes are strong growers and take up a lot of space so although you could grow one in a small house the chances are you would grow very little else!

588 *Cannot they be controlled in size to take up only part of the house?*

This is possible, though you won't get quite as good results as if they were able to develop fully. The trouble is that as years go by, the plants tend to get more and more vigorous and take up more space. It is a hard-hearted gardener who can cut back severely a well developed, vigorously fruiting vine!

589 *Could I perhaps grow one in our home extension, which is a kind of conservatory with glass sides and a translucent plastic roof?*

Yes, this is a good idea. A sitting-room with a growing vine is most appealing.

590 *Can I grow vines in a greenhouse without artificial heating?*

This is certainly possible, provided that your area of the country gets enough warmth and light late in the season to ensure that the grapes actually ripen. It is fairly easy to get fruit to set; it is ripening which takes time and which may prevent success in the North.

591 *What is the best method of growing grapes?*

By putting them into a really well prepared border, deeply dug with first-class soil and a well balanced fertiliser content. However, this is not really practical for small greenhouse work.

592 *Why not, if it is the best method?*

The root being within the greenhouse and in such favourable conditions will spread rapidly and take up all the available space!

593 *Is this the reason why many gardeners plant their vines outside the house and guide the stem inside?*

Yes. It also makes watering easier as the outside roots will, of course, be soaked by natural rainfall and the drainage from the greenhouse roof.

594 *Will the roots require protection in winter?*

They are best covered with straw or sacking during severe spells.

595 *I am putting up straining wires to support my vines. How far from the glass should these be placed?*

About 18in.

596 *If a vine is planted outside the greenhouse what soil preparation is needed?*

Dig down at least 3ft and try to get some old turf to put in the bottom of the hole (it is even worth buying a few pieces of lawn turf). It will rot slowly and serve the vine well over the years.

597 *What else is added above this turf?*

Vines like phosphates, often derived from bone in the form of bone-meal.

A useful long-term tip is to bury in the filling soil a few pounds of actual broken bones. Mix these in with ordinary fertile topsoil.

598 *Will lime be needed?*

About half a bucket per plant of coarse lime rubble, well turned in, is useful except where the soil is already very alkaline (limy or chalky).

599 *My soil borders are not very well drained. Will this affect the plants at all?*

Vines detest being in damp, stagnant soil. Try to improve the drainage by some of the methods described elsewhere.

600 *How old should the young plants be when they are finally put into place?*

Two, or preferably three years.

601 *What spacing is required?*

One vine is usually enough. It you intend to grow several sorts, keep them at least 1yd apart.

602 *When are vines usually planted?*

Autumn or winter, though since they are usually supplied in pots you can actually move them at any season without risk.

603 *How big should a good young vine be?*

Usually about 8ft long, but provided it is healthy the exact size does not matter much. In any case, it will be pruned down after planting.

604 *How much early pruning does a vine need?*

This depends on the precise type of greenhouse. Growth will start from the topmost bud left after pruning. This should be just high enough to receive direct light from the south.

605 *So if the greenhouse has side walls—say 3ft high—the plant will be cut short about 3½–4ft high?*

Yes. No more than that. Of course where the glass goes to ground level the plant will be much more severely shortened—down to 18in or so.

606 *Won't such severe pruning affect its growth?*

Yes, but only for the better. The most vigorous growth springs from buds on stems that have been pruned hard beforehand and you want rapid and healthy growth to make the best of your vine.

607 *When is this first pruning done?*

The spring after planting.

608 *Are vines planted very deeply?*

No, the soil covering should only be 1–2in deep over the topmost roots. Make sure, though, that they are firmly held.

609 *When can I expect fruit from a newly planted vine?*

Certainly not in the first year, and only a limited amount in the second.

610 *How is fruiting prevented—by cutting off the trusses after they have formed?*

It is better to start at the flowering stage and not to allow any development of fruit at all. This will concentrate the plant's attention on developing a strong stem system.

611 *Will the vine require special heating or treatments which will interfere with the growth of other plants?*

It would if you wanted to get the very best results. In fact though, you can get good grapes in most parts of the country simply by allowing the vine to grow in the usual temperatures that your tomatoes, for example, require. After all, the tomato is really the more important crop!

612 *To get early grapes, what special attention would be needed?*

Very careful control of the heat, starting at 45°F (7.2°C) during the early part of the season.

613 *What temperatures are required later?*

The maximum is 70°F (21.1°C) during the flowering period. After that a slight lowering is allowable down to 63°F (17.2°C) to 67°F (19.4°C). This should be maintained until the fruits are completely ripe.

614 *Are vines very tender and delicate?*

No. They will withstand a good deal of rough treatment. In fact, a common amateur mistake is to be too weak with the pruning. This should be really drastic, in the midwinter especially.

615 *Is the pruning of mature vines difficult?*

Not really, since in small greenhouses only a single main rod is kept.

616 *How is this ensured?*

As the plant develops each spring, several growths will start. Choose the strongest of these and guide it into place, removing the others.

617 *What happens later?*

Side shoots will spring out. These are reduced in number as growth develops to one every 12in.

618 *What pruning is needed after the fruit starts to form?*

Pinch off the shoot beyond each truss, leaving two leaves beyond to draw sap past the fruit.

619 *How far apart should fruiting side shoots be arranged?*

Aim to have one side shoot for each foot of main stem. Pull them down to your straining wires and tie them carefully in place.

620 *Should the side shoots be trained up the ridge or along the length of the house?*

Along the house length, at right angles to the upright rod.

621 *Is summer pruning ever done with grapes?*

After the fruit has been taken, it is customary to shorten the side shoots that have carried them by about half, and then in winter complete the pruning back to the basal buds.

622 *I have a vine that has grown right over the top of my span-roof house in its first year. Should I cut it short at the ridge?*

No, much further down. Letting it reach up to the ridge at this early stage will only weaken later growth. The rule is in the first season to prune back to one third of the vine's growth —9ft of new stem being cut back to 3ft.

623 *When is this done?*

In very late autumn or winter. Do not leave it till the buds start growing in spring.

624 *In the second year, how much pruning is done?*

This depends upon the health and the thickness of growth that has developed. Your aim is to produce a stout rod that will throw out vigorous side shoots. If the second year growth is at all weak it is best to cut it back again by rather more than half and let another season thicken its base.

625 *What do I do with the side shoots that have grown out from the main rod?*

In both mature and young plants, prune all these back very close to the main stem. Near their bases you will find a number of tiny buds. It is from these buds that next year's side shoots will develop.

626 *I am told that grapes have to be thinned. Is this really essential?*

Most grape bunches contain far too many berries. It is as well to reduce these by half to allow them to be spaced about 1in apart.

627 *When is this done?*

When they reach $\frac{1}{4}$in in diameter. Be delicate, using long bladed scissors.

No two grapes should be left touching each other.

628 *Will watering or feeding be required?*

Water must be given, as with all greenhouse plants, to ensure a moist atmosphere. Liquid manures are useful when the fruits are developing.

629 *Since grapes need heat as well as humidity, ventilation must presumably be limited?*

On the contrary, ventilation is very important indeed. Grapes will not do at all well in a hot, muggy atmosphere. They require a constant flow and change of air. This is more important than excess heat.

630 *How can I achieve moist growing conditions with such ventilation?*

The ideal is frequent spraying with a fine spray.

631 *Is ventilation important for any other reasons?*

Yes, disease is very much more likely in humid, still conditions. Also, excessive heat may build up in sunshine, resulting in damage to the leaves and developing fruits.

632 *How much artificial heat will grapes require?*

It depends on whether you are aiming for early crops. The earlier the fruit, the more heat is called for.

633 *How difficult would it be, say, to produce crops in early spring?*

You must have the vines growing on well by November in a temperature of of about 60°F (15.6°C) and this must rise still higher when the flowers appear.

634 *This sounds to be a very expensive matter!*

It is. These days, forcing grapes is not a profitable occupation for the home gardener.

635 *Can I go a little way in forcing to have them, say, in early summer?*

You can get grapes in July if you bring on the heat in February, reducing it as the days lengthen and warm up.

636 *How much heat do unforced vines require during winter?*

Hardly any. They will even withstand a very slight frost. Of course, a severe degree of frost must be prevented.

637 *Do some vine varieties require more heat than others?*

Yes, varieties do differ and a chat with your nurseryman could produce some useful information. In particular, Muscat type grapes often need considerably more heat than others.

638 *Will vine flowers need pollinating by any artificial means?*

Not always, especially in sunny weather, and if the vinery is well ventilated. It is as well, though, not to spray with water during the flowering time as this might stop the pollen from being blown about.

639 *I have seen some gardeners tapping the rods at this time. Does this help?*

This is useful, especially in overcast

weather when the pollen might not distribute itself naturally. Go along the vine and shake it gently.

640 *What diseases attack vines?*

More vine troubles are brought about by bad culture than by disease attack!

641 *What type of defects should I look for?*

If the leaves shrivel up and seem scorched, it probably means bad ventilation or possibly waterlogged soil.

642 *The stems of my young grape vine shrivel up. What disease is this?*

If the vine is young it is probably because you are taking too many bunches from it. Next year, reduce the number allowed and this should result in a big improvement.

643 *I have had the same trouble on a mature vine. Is there any way I can cure it?*

Overcropping is still the problem, but with older vines it is overcropping in relation to the food producing capacity of the roots. Your best bet would be to dig under one side of the vine and re-embed the roots there in fresh soil.

644 *How exactly is this done?*

Dig and crumble the soil away from all the side roots and lift clear the spreading ones near the surface. Cut through thick ones that strike deeply downwards. Re-embed the selected roots in good, fresh soil brought in from elsewhere.

645 *I was told by an old gardener to cut notches in old roots without actually taking them off. What effect does this have?*

Notching of roots used to be practised sometimes when a vine was not doing very well. The coarser roots were exposed and notches halfway through made on their undersides at intervals of 4–5in. After re-embedding in fresh soil, new 'feeder' roots would soon develop from these notches. This did often have a good effect and you can certainly try this if you have got a valuable old vine that is looking unhappy.

646 *My vines seem to be attacked by a small insect that leaves stuff like wholemeal flour dusted along the stems and leaves.*

This is probably mealy bug and is a serious pest. Insecticide treatments on the plant itself can give a temporary respite until winter. Even water spraying can help, using a fine but powerful spray.

647 *What should be done in winter?*

Paraffin is the traditional remedy for mealy bug and is scrubbed all over the woodwork where the bugs over-winter. Old vines should have their bark carefully sprayed with insecticide to get at hibernating insects. The following season, make sure that top spraying with water is continued as this washes the insects down on to the soil where they are less of a trouble.

648 *What treatment is given for an attack by red spiders?*

Top spraying here, too, is very effective as the red spider only likes dry conditions.

649 *Can I use insecticide sprays to help?*

Yes, but not when the grapes are actually developing. Once they start to swell, plain water is the best thing to use.

650 *I suppose it is best to hold the pipe up in the air and let the spray fall like rain on to the leaves?*

No, the exact opposite. Use a high pressure spray and apply it from underneath, so that any clinging insects are washed away from the underside of the leaves where they often rest.

651 *Many shoots and fruits on my vine are covered with white mould. How can I treat this?*

First improve your house ventilation. Mould develops in a stagnant, cool, moist atmosphere. You may be over-doing the watering without providing an adequate air flow.

652 *Is there any chemical treatment as well?*

Sulphur is a powerful and effective fungicide. You can get it in dust or spray form. Follow the instructions given by the makers.

653 *Is there any way of dealing with wasps that attack the grapes?*

Only by keeping them out of the house by porous cloth, such as muslin, over the doors and ventilators.

654 *How are grapes normally propagated?*

From buds, although sometimes cuttings are used.

655 *How can single buds be used for propagation?*

Take off a length of side shoot with several undeveloped but plump buds (usually called 'eyes'). Select the fattest of these and cut through the stem on both sides, to give pieces about 1in long. Place these 2–3in apart in a large pot of compost.

656 *What type of compost is best for vine propagation?*

A peaty or leafy one. If you can get leaf mould from a beech wood use this with an equal part of medium soil and a handful of coarse sand to each 6in pot.

657 *Will they require heat to develop roots?*

Only to a small degree. In the greenhouse or even a warm room they will usually root quite well and the bud will push out tiny leaves.

658 *How are vine cuttings prepared?*

From side shoots taken with a 'heel'. This means that a side shoot is pulled away from its parent stem with a bit of the parent stem's bark still attached.

659 *How long are the cuttings?*

Five or six buds long (you will find these buds spaced out along the shoot).

660 *Are all the buds kept intact?*

No. Only the top two are left in place. Rub the others off.

661 *How deeply should I insert the cuttings?*

So that the second bud from the top is just above soil level.

662 *How successful are plants grown by amateurs from cuttings or eyes?*

They will certainly grow and be true to type, but of course it does take some years to develop good sized plants. Grow about twice as many as you actually need, then select the best to keep.

Leeks

663 *Can I get early crops of leeks by sowing them under glass?*

This certainly helps. Your seedlings can then be put out (into prepared trenches) as soon as the weather in your area allows. You may gain four or five weeks this way.

664 *What is the earliest reasonable date for sowing?*

February, in areas that are free of frost by March. Always keep a few seedlings growing, in case frost does wipe out your first transplants!

Lettuce

665 *What is the simplest method of growing early lettuce?*

Rake down a border in a cool house or frame. Sprinkle the seeds over and lightly cover them. As seedlings develop, thin them to 1–2in apart. As they grow further, plants 2–3in high can be picked to eat till the remainder are 9in apart.

666 *Are there varieties specially suited to greenhouse or cold frame growing?*

Yes, and you can ask for these from your nurseryman. Cheshunt Early Giant was a well known one which gave good results in warm houses, but every year sees the introduction of new varieties.

667 *Can I get lettuce all the year round from a greenhouse?*

Not easily in every area, since lettuce requires plenty of light. This makes it harder in the North.

668 *What is the season through which northern gardeners can grow them?*

Usually you can get crops in the North from early April to the end of June.

669 *Are there varieties for such cold areas too?*

Yes, there are some which do not require a very bright, long day to develop.

670 *How are lettures normally sown for greenhouse culture?*

Mostly in boxes of seed compost or in a succession of fairly large plant pots.

671 *You surely won't get many seedlings in a pot!*

More than enough for a successon. It is better to grow lettuce in several batches of twenty or thirty plants to mature after each other. If you plant more together you will have a large crop all ready at the same time.

672 *When are the seedlings planted out?*

If you are growing them in the border they can be put out as soon as they can be handled—even only about 1in tall.

673 *What cultivation is needed in the borders?*

Make sure the soil is of fine rich texture. Lettuce must make rapid growth so they need good soil.

674 *Will lime be needed?*

Bring the soil to a pH of 6.5 for best results.

675 *What about fertilisers for young lettuce?*

You can give these during the preliminary digging by using your tomato fertiliser at ½lb per square yard.

676 *A friend of mine recommends putting the plants out into pots before putting them in the border. Is this a good plan?*

If you've got the space and time it certainly helps the seedlings to develop a good root system. If you pot up rather more than you need you can then select the best grown plants. Peat pots are best because plants in them can grow on unchecked, the whole pot being 'planted'.

677 *How much watering is given on planting?*

The soil must be moist and kept moist by fine spray as the first few leaves start to develop.

678 *When is the best time for watering?*

Very early morning. Wet plants lose heat rapidly at night, which is undesirable.

679 *How close are lettuce planted out?*

6–7in apart is enough for small sorts. When using big varieties and there is ample light, 8–9in is not too much.

680 *What temperature must the greenhouse be for lettuce?*

Not very high. Only 45°F (7.2°C) to 55°F (12.8°C).

681 *Is a higher temperature harmful?*

Try to control the upper level at no more than 70°F (21.1°C) or you may find the lettuce do not heart up well.

682 *Can I grow lettuce before putting in my tomatoes?*

Yes. This is commonly done and a very good practice. However, remember that lettuce extract foods from the soil which need replacing just before you put in the tomatoes.

683 *How is this best done?*

A simple application of 2oz of hoof and horn meal once the lettuce has been removed will be satisfactory.

684 *Are lettuce subject to many diseases?*

Fortunately, not many. Botrytis disease is one, so many gardeners use a proprietary dust just before planting to discourage it.

685 *I have tried growing lettuce but many of them failed through a kind of grey mould. How can I cure this disease?*

It is better to prevent it. The cause is almost certain to be poor ventilation, perhaps caused by watering early in the morning and failing to open the ventilators afterwards to allow the

95

leaves to dry off. Throw away those plants that are too far gone but try opening the vents all day, which might cure the problem for the rest. Sulphur dust or sprays help too.

Melons

686 *How long does it take to grow melons from seed?*

On average you can cut melons seventeen weeks from sowing.

687 *Are melons difficult to grow?*

No. Certainly no more difficult than cucumbers.

688 *When is the work best started?*

Seed is sown usually in March or April, but earlier seeding is possible.

689 *What is the planting method?*

Slide one seed into each small pot on its edge.

690 *What type of pot is best?*

It is important for melons to grow ahead rapidly. Peat pots are therefore best initially because they remove checks on transplanting.

691 *What type of compost should be used?*

If you are using John Innes types, the No 1 is best. Avoid stronger kinds.

692 *How many plants will be needed?*

Like cucumbers, melons grow vigorously. Only one or two are likely to be required.

693 *When will they be ready for*

planting out on to the stages or in borders?

Four to six weeks after seeding.

694 *Will they need potting up further, after the initial potting?*

They can be moved into 5in pots as soon as they have developed well.

695 *Are they stopped or pruned whilst in the pots?*

For greenhouse work leave the leading shoot, but take all side shoots out.

696 *How big should the plants be when they are finally put in the border?*

About 12–15in tall, with several large, rough leaves.

697 *I want plants for frames, and such plants are rather large. Should I stop off the leading shoots earlier?*

For frame use the procedure is different. The main leading shoot should be taken out after two or three rough leaves have formed and all side shoots left in. These can then spread out over the flat soil of the frame.

698 *What soil preparation should be done on the beds?*

Melons like a well drained position so it is common to heap the soil up into a mound about 2ft high. Make sure it is well cultivated and treated, ideally, with farmyard manure.

699 *Will the soil require any further chemicals?*

You can use your tomato base fertiliser (not the high potash type).

This will provide most of the additional fertiliser required. About ½lb per plant would probably be adequate at first.

700 *I cannot get any rotted farmyard manure. Can I simply use a richer compost?*

You could use John Innes No 2 in this case.

701 *Presumably the plants are put at the top of each mound?*

Yes. Make sure the soil is moist and that the atmosphere is kept humid with a fine spray.

702 *How much warmth will be needed?*

Melons are fairly tolerant of a range of heat but prefer something rather like cucumbers, about 55°F (12.8°C) to 65°F (18.3°C) minimum.

703 *Will the plants continue to require pruning or training?*

The usual method is now to take out the leading shoot so as to force the growth of several vigorous side branches. These can then be fan-trained along wires or a cane frame-work. Some growers with limited space just retain the leading branch making a tall, narrow plant.

704 *They seem to be rather a trouble. Is all this pruning really necessary?*

You can get crops without so much pruning, simply by stopping all the shoots when the plant's size has filled the space available.

705 *Must the male flowers be removed, as in cucumbers?*

No, melons must be fertilised. They have both male and female flowers.

706 *What is the difference between them?*

Like cucumbers, the female has a tiny fruit behind it.

707 *How is this fertilising done?*

By hand, pulling off the male flowers and pressing these into the female flowers.

708 *How many fruits will I get on each plant?*

You may get quite a number but you ought to reduce these to four or five, well spaced out. The mature size varies with variety and cultivation skill, but small or medium sizes are often tastier.

709 *Are the fruiting shoots shortened?*

Yes, pinch them off two leaves beyond the fruit.

710 *I have seen melons hung in little string nets. Is this desirable?*

Yes. It is always as well to have the great weight of the developing melon supported by nets (which are themselves attached to the supporting framework), otherwise the weight of the fruit causes them to rest on the soil and often produces rot.

711 *How can I tell when melons are ready for picking?*

Their sweet smell is unmistakable.

712 *How much watering will be required?*

It is vital to maintain good growing conditions with a suitably moist atmosphere. Give a twice daily sprinkling of the soil and sufficient air humidity should be maintained.

713 *What about feeding?*

Regular feeding with liquid manure every week should certainly be practised, until the fruit has reached its full size.

714 *Are canteloupe melons (the rough-skinned, orange-flesh type) also easy to grow?*

Yes, these sorts are started in the greenhouse and later put out into cold frames for growing on. They are an excellent way of improving the usage of a range of frames, and of course save valuable greenhouse space.

715 *Is there any difference in their cultivation?*

Very little, except that the developing melons must be protected from resting on the soil in some way, perhaps by providing boards underneath them.

716 *I grew melons successfully one year but the second season found them rather tasteless. Could this be some fertiliser deficiency?*

More likely the first year was brighter. Melons' flavour develops much more in sunny conditions. They most not therefore be shaded, by other plants for example.

Mint

717 *How can I get year-round mint?*

As the summer ends, dig up some of

the younger roots of your mint patch and plant them in boxes.

718 *Where are these placed in the greenhouse?*

Unlike many plants being forced, mint likes the light, so water the boxes well and raise them on shelves as near to the glass as possible. New shoots will soon develop.

719 *Can other herbs be forced similarly?*

Yes. Chives and tarragon respond well to winter forcing.

Mushrooms

720 *I have heard that mushrooms are temperamental and not always easy to grow. Is this true?*

Not really. If you take sensible care in the preparation of the compost and planting places you ought to get at least some crop every time.

721 *What average weight of crop am I likely to get?*

Much depends upon the exact conditions, so the range is fairly wide from about ¾lb up to as much as 4lb per square foot.

722 *Over what period can mushrooms be harvested from a single planting?*

For about three months.

723 *How many crops of mushrooms can be obtained throughout the year?*

Three, or even four, though for winter growing you will need a certain amount of heat.

724 *I keep my greenhouse only moderately warm in winter. What is the temperature needed for a good mushroom crop?*

Mushrooms prefer cool conditions provided that the temperature does not drop below about 40°F (4.4°C) to 45°F (7.2°C). Even frost will only set back the mushrooms, slowing down their development. The maximum temperature for first-class quality should be about 55°F (12.8°C). Where higher temperatures are expected, ventilation (which is always important) becomes vital.

725 *How difficult are they to grow inside the house?*

Mushrooms can be grown in any well ventilated place where there is not too wide a range of temperature. They do not grow well if the room becomes too warm.

726 *Why is ventilation so important if temperatures remain stable?*

Failure to ventilate increases the carbon dioxide content of the air. When this rises above 5 per cent, growth of the mushrooms slows down or may stop.

727 *Would mushrooms growing in a house create an unpleasant smell?*

Not with properly made compost. This does not smell in its preparatory stages but this is done outside. Once the fermentation necessary to make the compost is completed, the smell is greatly reduced and indeed most people find it quite pleasant.

728 *When growing mushrooms indoors, surely watering must present a problem?*

Mushrooms should never be watered so much that moisture runs out of the boxes. If this happens it is a sure sign of overwatering and is very bad for the crop.

729 *What sorts of places might suit mushrooms?*

Any empty room, whether light or dark (though mushrooms beds are best out of direct sunlight); a cellar; under stairs; in garages and, of course, in garden sheds; cold frames or under the staging in your greenhouse.

730 *I have some old stone outbuildings. Could these be made suitable for mushroom growing?*

Render them free from draughts by blocking up holes and, preferably, by lining the interior with cement to give a smooth surface in which pests and diseases cannot easily lodge. Each year you will have to fumigate any building and if there are inaccessible crannies the gases may not reach them. A lining of polythene is a fair substitute and relatively cheap.

731 *I thought mushrooms were best grown in the dark?*

Wild mushrooms grow happily in the fields. Darkness is not necessary. The reason for keeping sunshine off mushroom boxes or beds is to prevent the surface soil caking hard and impeding the growth of the mushrooms breaking through. However, dark places do tend to have more even temperatures, day and night.

732 *They must take up a lot of floor space to get a good crop?*

You can stack boxes above each

other with 6in gaps between for watering and for the crop to develop. One wall of a garage could accommodate a dozen or more boxes.

733 *How big should the mushroom boxes be made?*

The exact area does not matter but they should be 8–9in deep. Many growers use fish boxes (about 3ft by 2ft) which you may be able to obtain from your local fishmonger.

734 *If I make up my own boxes, what sort of timber should I use?*

Any sort of tough timber, the ideal being cedar, which requires no preservative but will never rot. It is, though, expensive and weaker than other woods so needs to be fairly substantial, 1in thick at least. Look also for second-hand wood which can often be obtained from demolition contractors. Floorboards ¾in thick are good. It is important, however, to treat this wood against rot by a thorough painting with copper-based wood preservative.

735 *Is creosote a suitable wood preservative?*

No. Never use it under any circumstances. Mushrooms will not grow in close contact with creosote, tar, bitumen or similar material.

736 *I have been told that you need lots of farmyard or stable manure to grow good mushrooms. Is this necessarily true?*

No, there are other materials such as plain wheat straw. Indeed, you often get fair crops in a mixture of ordinary garden soil and peat.

737 *Is making up the compost hard work?*

No. It is usually quite light, often consisting mainly of straw, manure and perhaps a little fine soil.

738 *What are the simplest basic materials for amateurs to use?*

Wheat straw, poultry manure and chemicals (though you can, at a pinch, do without the manure).

739 *Will any other sort of animal manure serve?*

Yes, farm or stable manure, provided it is fresh.

740 *When starting out in mushroom growing, how many trays should I prepare?*

It is probably best to start with only half a dozen trays, to gain experience.

741 *How much compost will be needed for these?*

1cwt of wheat straw, about 14lb of poultry manure (or similar), 7lb of pink gypsum (bought from builders' merchants) and roughly 7lb of a commercial activator.

742 *What purpose does the activator serve?*

It is specially prepared to start off the rotting process. Most manufacturers enclose full instructions on the quantities needed.

743 *Do I use any soil in the mixture?*

Not at your first attempt, because there is always a chance of introducing mushroom disease.

744 *How is the compost prepared? I understand it is a long process.*

It takes a week or two, but the amount of time involved overall is not very great. Get all the materials together first and then find a smooth area to work on, preferably concrete rather than earth.

745 *Is it better to mix it outdoors or indoors?*

Indoor mixing is best, in a cool shed or garage. Outdoors the wind tends to dry out the compost rather quickly. If you must work outside give shelter if possible.

746 *Which parts of the materials are mixed first?*

Start with the straw. Work some out into a loose layer about 25 sq ft and 1ft deep. Then wet it thoroughly with a can or hose spray. It should absorb quite a lot of water. Over this layer of straw, sprinkle a handful of gypsum, a trowelful of activator, and a similar amount of poultry manure.

747 *Are these then mixed in?*

No. Leave them as a layer, adding another 1ft deep layer of straw on top. Place a second layer of gypsum, activator and manure and continue adding more materials until the heap is about head high.

748 *How is the heap finished off?*

If outdoors, round off the top of the heap so that rain is cascaded towards the sides. Indoors it can be left flat.

749 *Should I cover the heap in any way?*

Moist sacking over the top will help, or even a piece of polythene. Do not seal the heap completely with polythene, though, as fermentation needs air. To prevent the heap drying out from steady winds, provide screens too on the windward side.

750 *What will now happen to the heap?*

Fermentation will start at once and within two days the heap will begin to get hot. It will then have settled by 1ft or more. In four days the heap should have reached a temperature of about 160°F (71.1°C).

751 *How can I check this?*

Ideally, get a soil thermometer which can be thrust into the heap itself. You can fairly easily feel the temperature by hand, but of course this is much less accurate.

752 *What is the next stage of actual work?*

After six days or a week the heap has to be turned. This simply means shaking the whole heap out, mixing it and well watering any parts which appear dry. Don't overdo this watering, though, or you may wash out the activating chemicals. Aim for all parts of the mix to be evenly moist, but not running wet, a regular mixture of straw, activator and manure. Take great care with this first turn.

753 *Does this mean that more than one turn is done?*

Yes. After another week the second turn will be required. The compost will now have turned brown and will start to smell of mushrooms. You may still need a little water on this turn.

Two further turns will probably be needed at intervals of a week by which time the compost will have turned a rich mahogany red, rather dark but never black, solid or greasy. It should be open in texture, hold together when squeezed, and break apart easily when tapped. If it is too dry (leaving no moisture on the hand when you squeeze it) then add a little water at this first stage.

754 What should I do if the mixture appears too wet or greasy?

Add a further 7lb of gypsum, well mixed in.

755 It seems that it will take about three to four weeks to make the compost. How often must this be done each year?

You will need fresh compost for every crop. A year round supply needs three or even four mixes. However, it is not really heavy work and actually a turn only takes about 1hr.

756 When should this composting be done?

The first time in the season is at the beginning or middle of March (depending on your area) after the worst of winter is over. The next will be in about August. If you have winter heat, composting for this crop should be done about November.

757 How are mushrooms actually planted?

First of all you must buy the commercial spawn. This is not really a seed. It consists of compressed blocks of the actual roots of the mushrooms (called mycelium). Some makers provide spawn in solid blocks, others in small granules. Every maker gives detailed instructions about the actual planting.

758 What is the usual procedure?

Break the spawn up into lumps roughly the size of a 10p piece. Press these into the compost 6in apart and about 1in deep.

759 How are the boxes filled with the compost?

Simply pile the compost to overflowing into the boxes, then press it down as firmly as possible especially into the corners of the box. Add more and more until the box is filled perfectly level with the sides. Good compression is important. You can even use a house brick to get the necessary pressure. The compost will still be warm and may shrink slightly over the following weeks.

760 When is the planting actually done?

It is probably simplest at first to do it as soon as the boxes are prepared. Experienced growers wait for optimum temperatures but this is a delicate matter to determine.

761 What is done after planting?

Make the compost firm again and cover with sacking or polythene sheet to prevent it drying out. Certainly keep out direct sunlight.

762 Will the boxes need watering at all?

Never water the compost after spawning. If the water gets to the spawn it will die.

763 What is the next stage in growth?

In a temperature averaging about 50°F (10°C), three weeks will see the compost filling with a mass of grey threads of mycelium. Once this development has taken place the next stage is to case the trays.

764 What is casing and why is it done?

Casing is simply covering the mycelium-filled compost with a thin layer of soil, within which the mushroom buttons will be supported as they develop. Without a casing, mushrooms tend to fall over and often do not develop very satisfactorily.

765 What material is best for casing?

It is best to use sterilised soil and garden peat mixed together 50/50. Make sure the peat is really moist.

766 Cannot ordinary garden soil be used?

You risk introducing disease. Since you will need such small amounts it should be possible to obtain some sterilised soil from a local nurseryman. Each box would only take about half a bucketful.

767 How deep is this casing layer spread?

Exactly 1½in. This is important. Level the compost first by filling in shallow depressions and then check as you lay the casing that the depth is correct.

768 If the boxes were filled, how can I put a 1½in layer on top?

By this time the compost will have shrunk considerably, and should be at least 1½in below the level of the box sides.

769 How compactly should the casing be pressed down?

Not too solidly. It must remain well drained. (Very fine soil tends to become solid: this is bad for the mushrooms.) The casing should not be airless but relatively crumbly and friable.

770 The casing on my boxes has become very dry, but you say that we must not water it?

Water must not be allowed to get down into the compost beneath. A fine syringing to dampen the surface should always be given if the casing appears to have dried out.

771 When will the crop appear?

About three weeks after casing. At this time you can spray a little more freely.

772 How are the mushrooms best picked?

By a gentle twisting action, since they grow in clusters and this leaves behind the smaller ones near the base. Once a clump has been completely cleared you can cut out the root with a sharp knife and fill the hole in with casing material. This will then rapidly fill with more mycelium to increase the crop.

773 In growing mushrooms I seem to get regular 'waves' of mushrooms every week or so, with intervals when there are very few. Is this normal?

Yes. Mushrooms crop in this way at roughly ten day intervals. This goes on for three or even four months with the crop gradually diminishing. Most of the crop is taken in fact during the first six weeks.

774 *What is done with the boxes afterwards?*

The compost is a valuable garden material and should be used as fertiliser. The boxes themselves must be sterilised by formalin or some other fungicide and then stood outside for some weeks before being refilled. This helps to cut down disease risks.

775 *Should I give any pest control?*

Various pests do attack mushrooms but prevention of attack is far better than cure. Prepare the compost correctly and see that it does in fact heat up substantially. This itself kills most pests. (The ideal—not easy to achieve by amateurs—is to maintain 145°F (62.8°C) in the compost heap for 48 hours.) BHC powder can be used to protect mushrooms from pest attack. It is most effective if you can seal up the place containing the trays for about half a day whilst the powder takes effect.

776 *Are there diseases which attack mushrooms?*

There are indeed, and once again it is far better to prevent than to cure it! One important factor is the use of sterilised soil for the casing material. Good ventilation too is vital.

777 *What general advice about disease control can you give?*

If your mushrooms appear to be unhealthy, deformed, discoloured or pitted in any way, it is far better to remove and clear that box, otherwise you risk the real possibility that the trouble will spread to all the boxes.

104

Oranges

778 *Can orange trees be grown successfully in a greenhouse?*

Yes, in a house with just enough heat to prevent frost entry.

779 *Where are they best planted?*

Oranges are customarily grown in tubs or large pots and overwinter in a conservatory. They like a 'holiday' outdoors in summer. You can actually get a bush in a 6–8in pot. However, the fruits may not be very large and pot plants are more for decoration than fruit.

780 *How can I get a larger fruit?*

By growing larger trees in bigger boxes, but the space they take up is considerable for the amount of fruit you get. However, they do make an interesting tree to have in a cool conservatory.

781 *Are any particular type of orange best?*

The Otaheite and Calemondin oranges are fairly hardy and decorative too.

782 *What sort of soil will the tree require?*

A standard compost (not too rich) will serve, particularly with extra peat added.

783 *Will any pruning be needed?*

Practically none, but keep turning the plant from time to time to promote regular growth.

784 *Will oranges require top spraying?*

This is desirable for most plants. You can also wash down an orange tree more vigorously from time to time to prevent dust clogging the leaf pores.

785 Can I grow orange trees from pips?

You can grow the tree but not the fruit as a rule. Stems of fertile fruiting sorts must be grafted on to a seedling stock plant.

786 Is this possible to do at home?

Yes, if you have one fruiting orange. You can graft one of its stems by a process called inarching.

787 How is this grafting done exactly?

Cut a downward slit halfway through the base 'trunk' of the pip grown plant. Stand the fruiting plant nearby. Cut short one of its stems and shape it to fit into the slit. Bind them both firmly, making sure that the exposed sappy green wood of both plants is pressed firmly together. In a month or two union will take place and then the fruiting branch can be cut clear of its mother plant and grown on.

788 What happens to the other part of the pip grown plant—its own natural branches?

When the grafted shoot has taken securely, these are cut away and the fruiting shoot trained upright.

789 Is there any way I can make orange trees bloom more vigorously?

They always do best if very constricted around their roots and the soil pressed very tightly round them. Delay repotting growing plants as long as possible and then do it in spring,

very firmly.

790 Can grapefruits also be grown and fruited?

We have not actually seen this done but believe that the treatment is similar to that given to oranges.

Parsley

791 Can parsley be cut all the year round?

Yes, if you have a warm frame. Frost is what prevents parsley developing.

792 When is seeding done?

Plants are usually started off outdoors. The main sowing is made in March or April.

793 Is parsley particular about its soil?

It will grow in most places but for best results a soil enriched with farmyard manure is desirable. Turn this in deeply and also give 4oz per square foot of superphosphate.

794 How deeply are the seeds covered?

Not more than ½in deep in rows. When the seedlings develop they can be thinned to 3–4in apart.

795 I put in parsley seeds one year but nothing came up. Could this have been a disease or frost attack?

It might have been, but the probability is that you were not patient enough. Parsley does take rather a long time to germinate.

796 Is it best to sow in a bright sunny

position?

No, shade suits parsley better, especially in sandy soils which tend to dry out under the sun.

797 *How can I get parsley in winter?*

Lift selected plants in autumn whilst leaves are still on, taking plenty of soil with them, and embed them in a deep tray which can be kept clear of frost in a cool greenhouse or frame.

Peaches and Nectarines

798 *Do peaches and nectarines need different culture under glass?*

No. The nectarine is merely a smooth-skinned and slightly more delicate version of the peach and its culture is the same.

799 *Is it possible to grow good fruit in all parts of the country?*

Peaches are remarkably hardy and can be grown outdoors. With the protection of a greenhouse you can crop them fairly easily as far north as the Midlands.

800 *What is the main difficulty with the amateur growing of peaches under glass?*

Simply the space needed. Even in good seasons the weight of fruit obtained per square yard of greenhouse space is not great. One peach per foot of fruiting stem is average.

801 *What is the best greenhouse type for peaches?*

The old-fashioned lean-to, where the trees can be grown in fans over the rear wall. Span-roofed greenhouses are not shaped really well for growing them, although you can train a fan up one of the ends.

802 *What type and age of tree should I buy?*

Three year old, partly trained into fan shape. Discuss the variety with your nurseryman, to make sure it is suited to indoor growth.

803 *When is planting done?*

Through winter and spring up to March at latest.

804 *What cultivation does the soil require?*

Trees are in position a long time. It pays to cultivate deeply, making sure that the border soil is really well drained and richly provided with natural manures.

805 *Is it true that peaches do well in a soil containing rotted-down turf?*

Yes, this is a well tried, traditional method. Obtain 2–3 sq yd of lawn turf. Stack it for two or three weeks till it starts to rot. Then take out a large planting hole, putting the turves, well chopped up, in the bottom. Little extra manure will then be needed.

806 *This does not seem likely to produce a very rich soil?*

No, but the texture will be excellent. Peaches on over-fertile soils often run too much to leaf and branch.

807 *How much heat is required by peaches?*

Not much, if you are content to get the

fruit at the normal summer season. Early fruit needs heat in late winter and spring.

808 *Presumably supports of some kind must be arranged?*

Yes. Permanent straining wires for attaching the branches are the best plan. Make sure these are really strongly attached to the wall in the first place. This will save a lot of trouble later.

809 *I understand the training and pruning of peaches is rather difficult?*

It need not be. The basic principle is simply to maintain a supply of new growth, to tie into fan position each year. Peaches fruit on new wood (shoots from the previous season), so you have to keep a constant fresh supply growing for the following year.

810 *My professionally trained young trees have the central stem bent over. Should I try to straighten this?*

No. If a central stem is allowed to develop upwards it will rapidly dominate the rest of the tree and ruin the fan shape and its fruiting. Always bend this leading shoot firmly to one side to restrict its growth. Many gardeners remove it altogether.

811 *How are young fans developed?*

Shorten each branch to one third in the spring after planting. From these shortened branches more shoots will grow during the year. Shorten these by half in the subsequent spring. In this way the branches multiply to form the typical fan shape.

812 *What about branches that grow outwards, away from the wall?*

Cut these away completely if they cannot be guided back flat. Nor should shoots be allowed to cross each other. There must always be enough space between the tips of the fan stems to allow for the development of fruiting shoots.

813 *Once the skeleton training is done, what regular pruning is required to encourage fruiting?*

Simply the selection of the best fruiting side shoots (vigorous growth is more common than weak growth). As above, prune away all young shoots springing outwards from the wall. Take out weakly ones, trying to leave a regularly spaced pattern of young shoots a few inches apart up all the main branches. These will then be ready to replace the older shoots that will now be bearing fruit.

814 *When is this done?*

In summer, as the fruit on the older shoots is ripening. Early work will save much trouble later.

815 *After the fruit has been harvested, what more pruning will be required?*

You will now have a tree consisting partly of older wood (which has fruited) and partly of selected young wood of the current season. Cut out all the old fruiting wood and tie into place enough new branches to completely cover the wall. These will bear fruit the next season.

816 *What about any side shoots on these new branches. Are these left in place?*

Leave one at the bottom and one at the top only. Rub off the rest.

107

817 *What happens to the one at the bottom?*

After the fruit has been gathered (the subsequent year) this bottom one will be ready to replace it.

818 *What purpose does the top shoot serve?*

This draws sap up along the length of the fruiting shoot.

819 *Are there any special pruning points to watch with mature peaches?*

Only to ensure that one or two new shoots are developed each season from near the base. Otherwise the bottom of the fans will become bare and unfruitful.

820 *When do the flowers first appear?*

Very early spring, even in February.

821 *Will they require pollination?*

Yes. Use a camel hair brush dipped from flower to flower several times over the flowering period.

822 *How much fruit should be allowed to develop? My peaches are setting well.*

Never more than one peach (or two nectarines) per square foot of fan.

823 *This means removing a large number of small fruits, which seems a pity.*

Yes, but the resulting crop will be very much better. In fact, you are quite likely to get just as much weight as you would if you left all the other ones to develop. Most of them would remain small and often rather tasteless.

824 *What are the main cultural requirements during the growing season?*

Moisture, coupled with good ventilation. Fine spraying daily is admirable, especially during sunny periods. The soil, too, must be kept reasonably moist.

825 *What temperatures do indoor peaches require?*

Not too high, especially in the early part of the year. A minimum of 45°F (7.2°C) at night should be maintained, but no more than 56°F (13.3°C) or 57°F (13.9°C) during the day.

826 *Should temperatures rise as the fruit develops?*

Yes, up to 65°F (18.3°C) or even 70°F (21.1°C) occasionally. But you must watch ventilation and see that temperatures do not rise too high.

827 *Can peaches be propagated, or grown from stones?*

Yes, this is possible but it is better for such an important fruit to buy ready grafted trees, from specially raised plants.

828 *What diseases attack peaches?*

Probably the commonest is leaf curl, when the leaves become yellow and often have red, swollen spots.

829 *Is control possible?*

Yes, lime sulphur or Bordeaux mixture at bud burst will control the worst of any attack.

830 *Some of my peach fruits are brown inside as if they had gone rotten. Is this a disease?*

Yes, brown rot. It is important to destroy immediately any fruits that are affected. Treatment cannot easily be given since it is too late in the season by the time it shows itself. Fungicide sprays early in the following season may help to prevent a recurrence.

831 *What about pests attacking peaches?*

Greenfly are often a nuisance. A winter wash of 5 per cent tar oil is most helpful at keeping the egg population down. Commercial insecticide sprays in summer can also be used. Such sprays control many small pests.

Pineapples

832 *Can I grow pineapples in a warm greenhouse?*

Yes, but it would not be worthwhile except as an interesting novelty! They need considerable heat and humidity and, even given these, only produce one fruit per plant. They take up quite considerable space.

833 *How is this actually done?*

Buy two or three good pineapples with the largest possible tops (see if you can get them before the greengrocer cuts away the upper part of the green top). Slice off the green complete with the top 1–2in of fruit. Plant this firmly in a well drained pot of good compost. Keep warm and moist and the leaves will develop, throwing roots out from the decomposing fruit below. Select the

best of these plants for growing on into progressively larger pots. The fruit forms eventually on a single central stem.

Potatoes

834 *How can I force early potatoes, say for Christmas?*

First start by sprouting the seed potatoes in late autumn in a light but frost-free place (this need not be warm). Once shoots appear the seedlings are ready for putting into the greenhouse.

835 *Are they put in boxes or pots?*

Either will serve. You can also put them directly into the soil of a warm frame.

836 *How many seed potatoes should I put into a pot?*

In an 8in pot—three. In a box 2ft by 1ft you can get about five.

837 *How deeply are they planted?*

2in. Be sure the pots have adequate drainage material and are kept evenly moist.

838 *Will growth be fairly rapid?*

Yes, there are few problems.

839 *How will I know when the crop is ready?*

Water the pots well and leave overnight to consolidate the soil. Invert the whole plant and tap it free of the pot. You can then examine the the root ball to see if potatoes have formed and pick off any that are large enough. Then carefully replace the pot, disturbing the remaining soil as little as possible.

840 *I can hardly do this with box-grown plants!*

With box or frame grown plants slide a fork underneath the plant and lift it gently to seek for tubers. Remove the whole plant when enough tubers appear to have formed.

841 *Can all this be done in the home, say in a glass home extension, or a bright storeroom?*

Yes. Anywhere that is light enough for the plants to grow normally. They make a novel houseplant in a decorative container!

842 *Surely the quantity gathered cannot be very great?*

No, but they are really delicious—a delicacy in their own right, to many people.

843 *Can I get really early outdoor crops of young potatoes by starting the plants off in the greenhouse and putting them outside later?*

Yes, you can gain several weeks in this way. The potato sets are simply planted in deep seedboxes, peat pots 3–4 in across, or indeed almost any other container with good drainage.

844 *Can I use ordinary garden soil to fill them?*

You will get better results with a fair quality compost such as John Innes No 2 or at least mix peat and garden soil 50/50 to produce a very light texture.

845 *When are these sets put in?*

You need a warm house at the very beginning of March. Keep the developing plants moist by fine overhead spraying.

846 *Do they need much heat?*

No, though they must never be frosted, nor must they risk frost when finally put outside.

847 *When is this transplanting out done?*

It depends on your region, of course, but generally some time in May. If there is still a frost risk, make sure that the plants are covered in some way every night. A few handfuls of straw are adequate for this.

848 *Is this the earliest that we can do such forcing?*

In a favoured district you could plant in January and put them out in April when the plants are already quite large. Some growers use 9in whalehide pots and start potatoes off in the beginning of the year. The extra pots are stood outside, the developing crop expanding to fill or even burst the pots.

849 *I tried this and the pots burst, exposing the tubers, which then turned green. Are these still edible?*

No. Green tubers are poisonous. Earth up round the pots to prevent light getting at them and they will not turn green next time.

Radishes

850 *Can I force radishes for early use?*

Yes, this is easy. You might also follow the old gardener's trick of mixing carrot and radish seed together, sprinkling it in rows in the frame, or even in boxes on a bright window sill.

851 How can I sort out the carrots from the radishes?

The radishes will mature much more rapidly. By the time they have been pulled out, the carrots will have room to spread.

852 Can I mix other vegetables in this same way?

Not quite, but in the same frame you might put ready-sprouted early potatoes.

Rhubarb

853 How easy is rhubarb to force?

Very simple indeed. You can be certain of good results (though the roots that you force will not be suitable for replanting later).

854 When is the work tackled?

Start in November by digging up the rhubarb crowns and leave them on the surface. (If you need replacement plants, cut off some side roots and replant them.)

855 How long are the forcing crowns left exposed?

Until frost has severely chilled them.

856 This seems a very drastic method!

Yes, but the idea is to persuade the rhubarb that winter has already passed and they can now start into growth again!

857 What is the next step?

Pack the roots in boxes surrounded by fine soil or peat and place them in a dark place under a greenhouse bench or in a shed or garage. Make sure that water can easily drain away.

858 Is much water required then?

Yes. The boxes must be thoroughly soaked and kept that way or the plant development will be restricted.

859 How much warmth will be needed?

Anything above freezing will give some growth but the greater the heat the faster and more lush the development.

Seakale

860 I have grown some seakale for its delicious blanched shoots, by sowing them outdoors two years ago. The crowns now seem big enough to force. How do I set about it?

It would pay to produce special crowns for forcing. Dig up some of your present plants and take off their side roots. Plunge these up to the tip 2ft apart in the spring (out-of-doors). You will get several shoots from the top of each root. Single these down to one per plant. These roots will be ready for forcing in autumn.

861 What method of forcing is used?

Pack the crowns closely with soil under the greenhouse stages. Cover them with black polythene to reduce light and keep them moist. Blanched leaves will then develop.

862 *How soon will they be ready for cutting?*

Seven to nine weeks.

863 *Can the roots be used again?*

No. Throw them away and grow more for next season.

Strawberries

864 *How can I use glass to produce early strawberries?*

The simplest method is to choose a couple of your best rows of outdoor plants and cover them with cloches throughout the early part of the year. You will gain two or three weeks in this way.

865 *What about the more elaborate methods, bringing them into the greenhouse for forcing?*

This is fortunately quite easy, though you have to plan the work and start in the preceding season.

866 *Are the plants simply dug up in autumn and brought into the greenhouse?*

No. You must follow a definite pattern, the aim being to persuade the plant that winter has passed and it is now time to fruit again.

867 *How is this done?*

Start by shifting some young runners from healthy mature plants into 3in pots in June. Sink these up to their

rims in the borders to let them grow on.

868 *These are not put into a cold frame then?*

Not until later. As they develop to fill the small pots shift them into 6in pots and then move them into a cold frame.

869 *What compost is used for these pots?*

John Innes No 2 or similar.

870 *Are the frames covered completely or open?*

Only the minimum shelter is required, the frames only being covered in really severe frost. From the plant's point of view this is the 'winter' and it will respond by settling down to a brief rest. When it is brought into heat later the plant will respond as if it were spring and start to flower.

871 *When is this done?*

In December or January put the plants into the greenhouse with a temperature of 45°F (7.2°C) to 50°F (10°C).

872 *Are they put on or under the stages?*

High up near the glass, in as light a position as possible.

873 *What about watering?*

They will not need any watering during the dormant period but when they are brought into the greenhouse make sure that the pot is adequately moist.

874 *When will the flowers actually appear?*

112

This will vary with the variety and the temperature. It may not be for two months or more.

875 *Presumably since strawberries fertilise themselves there is no problem here?*

Insects are scarce at this time and the plants will be protected from wind so it is best to do this by hand.

876 *How is fertilisation actually carried out?*

A dab of cotton wool into each of the flowers in succession will usually induce pollination.

877 *What is the main point to watch as the fruits develop?*

That although water is given it does not result in fungus diseases and the fruit does not rot. Support the developing trusses in some way, clear of the soil.

878 *How much fruit will they carry?*

It is best to limit the fruit to twelve per plant, nipping out the flowers accordingly.

879 *Is any manuring required at any stage?*

When the fruit is swelling, weak liquid manure twice weekly can be helpful.

880 *When will the fruit be ready?*

April or May, depending on the greenhouse heat and the exact variety you are growing.

881 *Is any pest trouble likely?*

Aphis (greenfly) may appear, but is easily controlled with Derris.

882 *Can the plants be used outdoors after forcing?*

They will survive if put out in spring, but it is probably better to grow new plants from young runners.

883 *Can the tiny wild strawberries be forced similarly?*

We have never tried, but there seems no reason why not.

Tomatoes

884 *Presumably tomatoes are very easy to grow since everybody seems to manage to produce them?*

You can certainly expect to get some results from tomato plants even in a rather badly run greenhouse. You will, though, get a lot bigger and often tastier crops if you know how to go about the job properly.

885 *What is the main limitation on growing tomatoes in this country?*

Tomatoes need a lot of light, especially in their early months, so the brighter, sunnier district you live in, the better crops you will get.

886 *What are the different methods of growing tomatoes?*

In the borders, in rings, on straw bales, in pots or in prepared 'Grobags' of compost.

887 *What is the simplest of all tomato growing methods?*

Buy ready-prepared bags of compost from garden stores, arrange them (as instructed with the bags) in your greenhouse and put ready-grown sturdy plants in them. The only disadvantage will be the cost of bags and plants, costs you can later save by growing plants from seed and preparing your own planting places and composts.

888 *I know that in border growing you put the plants directly into the soil. This seems the obvious method and must have many advantages.*

This is true. The plants can root as deeply as they wish and will be able to draw water and food from a large soil volume. This reduces problems of watering and feeding.

889 *What are the disadvantages?*

Tomatoes are subject to diseases which can build up in soils which are used year after year for the same crop. Grafted plants help, but are much more expensive.

890 *I have been told that plants in borders may grow too fast for their own good. What does this mean?*

Because of the large volume of soil available, giving almost unrestricted water and food, plants may produce leaves and branches rather than fruit. For complex reasons, plants can often be encouraged to produce fruit by restricting their growth, which is not easily possible in border culture.

891 *Is there any difference in harvest dates between border plants and those grown by other methods?*

Not a lot. Border grown plants may be slightly later in coming into fruit since the large volume of soil under a greenhouse may not warm up very

quickly in spring.

892 *Can I get tomato crops all year round?*

This is technically possible in a well organised, heated greenhouse. Whether it is economically desirable is another matter. The cost of heating for very early or very late fruit is considerable. It is probably best to restrict your programme to give you crops between April and late July.

893 *When is seeding done for the early crops?*

If you are aiming to pick in April you will have to sow in late November or early December. The seedlings will then be ready for planting out from the middle to the end of February.

894 *In our area the mornings and evenings are very dark at this time of year. Will this affect growth?*

Yes. You should only try for such early crops if you live in the South and and have a fairly long day in April. Of course, if you have an exceptionally clean, thin-framed greenhouse in a very light position you will have a much better chance.

895 *What about crops for May; when are they put in?*

Early December, and they will be ready for putting out in the house in late February or the beginning of March.

896 *Which is the earliest cropping month that a newcomer should aim at?*

Probably May. You can seed the

plants in December (if you have warmth) or you can, of course, buy young, ready grown plants.

897 *When will plants for May fruiting be available?*

From the middle of March.

898 *What about later fruiting crops?*

For picking in June you have to sow in February or put out plants in late April.

899 *What is the latest season we can get crops?*

It is best not to aim for later than July. These will be seeded in March and put out in the middle of May.

900 *Are all these dates suitable for any parts of the country?*

No gardener can work by the calendar! If you live in a warm, light area, have excellent facilities, a well constructed greenhouse and protection from north and east winds you can always gain a few days. With a shadowed greenhouse in an exposed situation, you will be well advised to wait. Indeed, in the far north you are not likely to grow anything except the later crops, simply because you will not have enough light in the early part of the year to develop young plants. All dates given therefore have to be considered as approximate only.

901 *How can I discover what dates are best for my particular area?*

Ask the advice of your local nurseryman (who may be supplying your plants) or consult friends and neighbours who already grow them. Find out what their success rate has been, when they put their plants in and also the varieties that do well.

902 *How are tomato seeds sown?*

Sprinkle them broadcast in trays of seeding compost, covering them with about $\frac{1}{4}$in of compost, lightly pressed down. Water the box from below after seeding and cover it with a sheet of glass and thin paper.

903 *What temperature will be needed?*

65°F (18.3°C). Try not to go higher as this may produce defective seedlings.

904 *When will the seedlings be ready for transplanting?*

Watch for germination, removing the paper covering as soon as they start to appear. Mostly seedlings can be transplanted 2in apart four days after the first leaves appear through the compost.

905 *I have seen tomato seeds carefully spaced in lines. Is this a good plan?*

Yes, with a spacing roughly 2in all ways. You will thus save yourself the job of later transplanting.

906 *Are seedlings spaced out further into trays or directly into pots?*

Either. Broadcast seedlings may be spaced out in boxes to grow on more. Spaced out seedlings can be put straight into 3–4in pots.

907 *Should these be of plastic or clay?*

Either material will do. Many gardeners prefer to move them into pressed fibre pots to avoid later transplanting problems.

908 *What about the use of soil blocks?*

If you can obtain or make soil blocks they are also a very good means of growing on tomatoes at this early stage.

909 *How are the potted seedlings treated?*

Keep them grouped together for easy control of warmth and watering. By half burying the pots in moist peat you can make a humid growing atmosphere around them which will bring them on rapidly.

910 *Which compost is used for the pots?*

John Innes No 1 is the best soil containing compost. With a soilless compost use the weaker 'seed compost' kind.

911 *What temperature must I maintain for the seedlings?*

The lowest night temperature should be 55°F (12.8°C) but do not allow the temperature to rise too much during the day or the plants may fruit too soon. Aim at about 65°F (18.3°C).

912 *Does this mean that lower temperatures actually speed up development?*

They increase the number of flowers developed, especially in the lower trusses. However, the process of ripening is also slowed, so nothing is gained.

913 *And how much watering will the young plants need?*

Never allow them to dry out. Naturally they don't want flooding or waterlogging either. As soon as growth is well established, start to space out the pots. Restricted light by shading from each other is very bad for young tomatoes.

914 *How much feeding will the young plants need?*

Tomatoes need continuous, uninterrupted growth for maximum performance. They should never be allowed to grow short of food. Always have on hand a liquid feed of what is known as 'high potash' content to apply if growth seems to be definitely restricted or hesitant.

915 *Is it better to give too much feed or too little?*

Never overdo it. Excess chemicals are more likely to damage the plant than too little.

916 *With the plants growing on, the time is presumably come for border preparation?*

The earlier this is completed the better. Try to get it done in midwinter or the end of January at the latest.

917 *What acidity is ideal for tomatoes?*

Aim for a pH of 6.5 (remember, more acid soils have a lower pH; less acid soils have a higher pH).

918 *Of the several kinds of lime, which is best for tomatoes?*

Ground limestone. If you cannot get this, choose hydrated lime rather than unslaked or slaked lime.

919 *A friend recommends me to flood the soil after liming. Is this desirable?*

Yes. In fact it is hard to overdo flooding at this stage. The water both distributes the lime and removes any excess salts in the soil. This is particularly important if you have had a soil analysis done which shows a high soluble salt content.

920 *What type of chemical fertilisers are commonly used with tomatoes?*

The main one is undoubtedly tomato base fertiliser (see questions 299–300).

921 *When is planting done?*

Not until the soil has reached 56°F (13.3°C).

922 *How is this temperature measured? Is a thermometer hung in in the greenhouse accurate enough?*

You can best measure it with a soil thermometer, which is most useful for greenhouse work and well worth its cost.

923 *Is is really important to get the temperature right?*

Yes indeed. Shifting tomatoes into soil colder than they are used to can weaken them considerably and leaves the plants open to attack by various diseases.

924 *How far apart should border plants be put?*

There is no hard and fast rule, the average being about 24in.

925 *I have been told that you can't plant tomatoes as closely in an east–west greenhouse as in one arranged north–south. Why is this?*

In the east–west greenhouse it is the southern side which will receive most of the sun. If you plant too closely on that side, those on the northern side get very little light. In such a case, space the southern plants rather more widely.

926 *I have friends who grow tomatoes much closer than this, down to 18in. Are they doing wrong?*

Not necessarily, especially for later crops. On the other hand, especially vigorous varieties or plants that have been grafted should never be planted less than 2ft apart or they will not have room to develop.

927 *How deeply should the plants be put in?*

At the same depth as they were in the pot. Many gardeners plant on a very slight mound to ensure that water does not stand around the base of the stem.

928 *How much water is given after planting?*

The soil should have been moistened the day before, and after planting very little water should be given. Usually, if you buy in plants already in pots, water them well an hour or two before planting (but not with very cold water).

929 *When putting in grafted plants, at what stage is either root removed— or are they both left on?*

In general, grafted plants with their two root systems are left entire on planting. Removing one of the root systems could give a severe check. The only time that a non-resistant variety root is removed is when wilt disease is present in the greenhouse (as known from previous years).

117

930 *Given that the soil temperature has to be 56°F (13.3°C), what air temperature is required on planting?*

Aim for not much less than 60°F (15.6°C) at night and 65°F (18.3°C) during the day.

931 *Is it better to have the greenhouse slightly too warm or too cool?*

It is most important during the day that the temperature should not drop below about 65°F (18.3°C).

932 *What is the maximum temperature that should be aimed at?*

About 75°F (23.9°C). Anything above this is likely to be undesirable.

933 *As plants get into growth, how much watering should be given?*

As little as possible. In fact, you should only water plants which look as if they need it, as shown by drooping of the leaves.

934 *This seems very harsh!*

It is vital to get the plants to push their roots out into the surrounding soil in their search for water. This will establish a good root system for later. Overwatering is a common amateur mistake with young tomatoes.

935 *I have seen gardeners spraying their tomatoes. Is this a good plan?*

A very fine spray over the leaves (not giving enough water to soak the soil) is fine when the weather is bright and sunny. Do not do this in dark or dull conditions.

936 *So watering must really be related to the weather?*

Yes, after the plant has established itself and is vigorously growing (up to 2–3ft) it will use up water roughly in proportion to the amount of actual light it receives.

937 *How much on average should be given per plant on a dark and dull day?*

About ½pt; never more than 1pt.

938 *What about showery weather, when sun and cloud alternate about evenly?*

In these conditions about 1½pt will be found correct.

939 *And in sunshine or very bright weather?*

Anything between 2–4pt per plant.

940 *So the average will probably be about a can of water per plant per week?*

This is about right, most plants will use 2 gal, but it must be emphasised that you have to relate the water intake to the weather conditions at all times for best results.

941 *How much feeding will growing tomatoes require?*

This is a question about which growers argue a good deal. You can have success with continuous feeding, with powders dusted over the soil or indeed with practically no feeding at all (at least during the first half of the plants' life). The tomato is very tolerant so success is possible with widely different feeding techniques.

942 *Can you describe the main techniques or methods which*

might be chosen?

Broadly speaking, these are firstly to give food in the watering water so that they get some every day; alternatively you can give a stronger liquid manure every week or powder fertilisers at about the same interval. Some gardeners feel that if you use plenty of farmyard manure and chemicals at the start, tomatoes should only be fed when they have used up a lot of the nutrients. This might be quite late on in summer.

943 *Is feeding started at any particular time?*

Usually when the first truss of fruit is established.

944 *This wide range of possibilities seems confusing. Can you give a specific plan which will give reasonable success to a newcomer?*

To be honest, this is not easy. Feeding tomatoes successfully depends on understanding the plant and seeing how it looks. For example, a plant showing very rich growth, long and leafy, probably needs more potash. Short, weakly plants probably need more nitrogen. Food needs vary with the variety, the original cultivation and indeed the weather! However, if you start the plants in well manured soil, you can leave them entirely until fruit starts forming. Then give standard liquid manure every week for a month. After that, increase to two or even three feeds weekly, according to plant growth.

945 *When do tomatoes normally need the most potash?*

Early on in the season and, as noted earlier, especially if the soil has been

sterilised by heat. High potash feeds should be given early if this has been done.

946 *When are the plants' nitrogen needs highest?*

Late in the season, after the nitrogen already provided in the soil has been partly used up.

947 *What is the usual season's plan, therefore?*

Start by giving high potash (if necessary), then standard, then high nitrogen foods late in the season.

948 *I prefer to feed with powders rather than liquids. How can I give the necessary potash and nitrogen?*

Early in the season give sulphate of potash at ½oz per square yard every ten days. After a month, start with a standard mixed tomato fertiliser, bought commercially.

949 *Is it just sprinkled over the surface or watered in?*

Always water in dry chemicals immediately and keep them away from the plants' stems or rot may be started.

950 *What powders can be used for giving additional nitrogen?*

1oz per square yard of sulphate of ammonia, nitroform or dried blood, if required.

951 *In ring culture of tomatoes, what spacing of the plants should be given?*

Very much the same as in borders. Anything between 18–24in.

952 *What compost is used for filling*

the rings?

Any of the standard composts but not a rich kind and not too quick-draining. For example, in the John Innes range, No 2 is better than the richer No 3. It is easy enough to apply more fertiliser if required later. In both cases (when mixing your own), leave out most of the usual sand in the mixture.

953 *How much water is given in rings after planting?*

The ring should have been watered the day before and then, provided the root ball of the young plant is moist, give a pint each. After this, do not give any further water.

954 *Do not ring-grown plants often need more water than border-grown plants?*

Yes, but they must get it from the ash layer. Keep the rings short of water at first even until the plant goes dark, bluish green. This will force it to seek water below.

955 *How long will this take?*

A week in bright weather, two weeks in dull.

956 *The main water being given in the gravel, how important is keeping the soil in the rings moist?*

This must be done in the following few weeks. Give about ½pt each, three times a week.

957 *How long does this go on?*

Until roots find their way down into the gravel beneath (check this by drawing aside the ash by the ring bottoms).

120

958 *I have been told that you should not water the rings at all later on. Is this correct?*

Many gardeners give all their water through the gravel beneath and only apply liquid manures into the rings. This is a very good method. However, manuring only starts when the first trusses start to swell. Until then, you must ensure that the ring compost does not dry right out. It is true, though, that it is better to underwater than to give too much.

959 *With what manures are plants in rings fed?*

The same as in the border, starting off with a moderately high potash and then moving gradually to a high nitrogen at the end of the season.

960 *Can I use the same chemicals as in border culture?*

Border liquid fertilisers are weak. You cannot apply so much liquid to a small ring. A more concentrated food is needed.

961 *Can you suggest a suitable mixture?*

4 parts nitrate of potash (agricultural grade), 7 parts magnesium sulphate, 5 parts of sulphate of ammonia and 10 parts superphosphate. Dilute 3oz in a 2gal can. This feed was, we believe, first recommended by the well known expert on ring culture, Frank W. Allerton. It gives excellent results.

962 *How much is given per plant?*

1pt, twice a week.

963 *How do I increase the potash supply early in the season?*

With regular feeding and a good original compost, without too much nitrogen, extra potash may not be needed. If the plant does grow too lushly to leaf and stem, dissolve 2lb of sulphate of potash in a 2gal can of water.

964 *This leaves a sediment in the bottom. Is this usable?*

No. Stir the mix for a day or two, then strain off the clear liquid. This concentrate is then diluted ½pt to 1gal before use.

965 *How much of this will each ring need?*

½pt. No more than two treatments should be needed. Later on, extra nitrogen may be given with a sprinkling of sulphate of ammonia.

966 *Why do ring grown tomatoes seem to produce earlier fruit?*

Restriction in root growth in the early stages tends to force the plant to develop fruit earlier.

967 *What is the main cultural difference then between ring and border growing, in the early stages?*

In borders it is easy to overwater; in rings it is easy to underwater (in the ash layer).

968 *What sort of supports are best for tomato plants in borders or rings?*

Some gardeners use canes but it is cheaper and just as good to use strings stretched from pegs driven into the soil up to the roof of the greenhouse (or to cross wires).

969 *I have seen gardeners tie the*

bottom of the string actually to the plant. Which is the best method?

You can tie a string loop round the base of the plant and carry the other end up to the roof. However, it is hard to avoid knocking the string from time to time during spraying operations and this gives a jerk to the plant. On the whole, it is better to use a driven-in peg to take the strain of the string at the base.

970 *Will the plants need tying?*

They will to canes, but with strings it is possible to make them twist round and support themselves.

971 *Do plants grown on straw bales need special cultivation techniques?*

Only in minor ways. Full details of this method are given in questions 407–34.

972 *At the junction between the leaves and main stem of my plants, shoots are developing. Should these be left on?*

No. You want a single central stem to tomatoes. Snap off every one of these side shoots as they appear.

973 *Why do some gardeners remove the bottom leaves?*

It is common for the lowest leaves of tomatoes to turn yellow and become diseased. These should certainly be snapped off, taken out of the greenhouse and destroyed. Leaf removal is also sometimes practised to allow the sun access to ripening fruit later in the season.

974 *I have seen some plants with almost every leaf removed. Is* *this desirable?*

Extremes like this should be avoided. The plant needs leaves to live healthily and this applies right to the end of the season. Removing healthy leaves should only be done when the plant is obviously making far too much growth or in order to allow sunshine to reach other plants. This can be needed on the southern side of east-west arranged greenhouses, as explained earlier.

975 *I find that the soil in my greenhouse rapidly dries out. I haven't the time to be continually spraying. What can I do about this?*

The simplest remedy is to spread 1–2in of crumbled peat moss over the entire surface of the border. Thoroughly wet this down. The water held in such a peat layer will keep the surface of the soil healthily moist for many hours, even in warm sunshine. It also encourages the development of surface-feeding roots.

976 *What things cause most trouble with tomatoes?*

Lack of system. They are very sensitive to regularity of feeding, watering and ventilation.

977 *Will too high or low temperatures affect growth much?*

Not so much in themselves, but if the range of temperature is too great, with very cold nights and very hot days due to defective heating or ventilation, this will certainly severely affect production.

978 *How can I tell whether this is happening?*

Leaves may curl up unpleasantly. A maximum/minimum thermometer will give the high and low temperatures reached.

979 *I am told that variation in heat can cause loss of fruit. Is this correct?*

Many things can cause tomato fruit to fail to set (though it is unusual for no crop at all to be produced). A large variation in day and night temperature is one of these factors.

980 *Do tomatoes set better if sprayed with the hormone setting sprays available today?*

Yes. Many growers use these as a regular routine to make sure of a set. However, spraying with plain water has a marked effect too and will usually work almost as well.

981 *How many trusses should I allow to set?*

Gardeners argue about this as well. In general, there is little point in stopping the growth of the plant until it has filled the greenhouse completely. Pinch out the growing point only when it is at about the highest point possible.

982 *When will this generally be necessary?*

At the end of summer, in August or early September.

983 *What should be done if the plant has not reached full height by then?*

You are not likely to get much ripened fruit after this anyway, so stop even a small plant at the same time.

984 *Can tomato plants be made into*

compost at the end of the season?

Yes, provided the compost heap is not near the greenhouse. Tomatoes, though not diseased themselves, may be carrying disease spores which can infect the air and ground for quite a distance. If in doubt it is better to burn the old tomatoes complete with as many of their roots as you can manage. At the same time, clean the greenhouse thoroughly.

985 *What diseases cause most trouble to tomato growers?*

Diseases are not the main problem. Many of the troubles called disease are, in fact, due to mistakes in growing. For example, fruit with a hard, black pit near the flower end (called blossom-end rot) is due to a water uptake problem.

986 *Is this commoner in ring culture than border planting?*

Yes. Sometimes roots fail to push down sufficiently into the ash bed. When watering of the rings themselves is curtailed, water starvation occurs, producing the problem.

987 *Can blossom-end rot be corrected?*

Increased watering in the rings and of the ash bed can sometimes correct the problem.

988 *I have some fruit that have almost circular light green patches round the stalks. What disease is this?*

Again, greenback is not a disease. Some varieties are troubled more than others, but the basic cause is poor or unbalanced feeding. Reduce nitrogen and increase potash, perhaps giving

sulphate of potash only, for three or four weeks, and the trouble may gradually disappear.

989 *My tomatoes have also developed patches and streaks of brown and white. Is this caused and cured similarly?*

Almost certainly. Good culture and careful feeding should prevent these defects.

990 *My tomato leaves have rolled themselves up lengthways, almost into tubes. They look very peculiar. How serious is this?*

Fortunately, this does not seem to affect the crop. The cause is over-powerful sap flow, often following too rapid and severe leaf removal.

991 *Many of my fruit split and bulge unpleasantly. Is this a disease that can be cured?*

Irregular water intake and feeding causes this. Too much sand in ring compost, causing rapid drying out between feeds, can produce it. More frequent watering and feeding will help. In borders, a 1in covering of moist peat will help to tide over plants between waterings.

992 *My tomato leaves are severely twisted and mis-shaped. Some are mottled. What disease is this?*

Virus infection. Remove and burn (not compost) the plants at once, before the disease spreads. There is no cure.

993 *My plants are in rings. What is the cause of the leaves changing in colour round the edges, as though they have been burnt? The effect*

started on the lower leaves and is now spreading up the plant.

Almost certainly the ash bed contains harmful chemicals. Flood it vigorously several times a week. If this fails to slow up the trouble, lift all the plants gently free of the ash. Lay them on thick polythene and spread 2in of peat round, well watered. They can then draw water from the peat till maturity.

994 *Must I then remove the ash bed?*

No. Regular flooding through the following winter will almost certainly clear away remaining impurities. If weed seeds germinate in the ash this is a sign that things are improving.

995 *My tomatoes have spots and streaks of dark coloured rot, and some fruit has actually fallen off. Can I cure this?*

Yes, provided the attack is in its early stages. The problem is botrytis, a common mould. Collect and burn all infected parts. Cut out with a razor blade all diseased sections of the plant, well back into healthy tissue. Paint all the cut surfaces with a liquid fungicide or powdered sulphur. Finally, cure the cause of fungus attack, which is poor ventilation. Open the doors in June and leave them open day and night. Too little ventilation is a common mistake in tomato growing.

996 *Although my plants have set a lot of fruit, they are covered with pale pimples, some with black spots.*

Again this is fungus attack. Use the same defences as for botrytis.

997 *Brown mould has appeared underneath the leaves. What cure is there for this?*

Spray with colloidal copper or Bordeaux mixture and prevent recurrence by improving ventilation.

998 *Are pests a serious problem on tomatoes?*

Only on plants already weakly from other causes. Virus disease can be carried by greenfly, but Derris or proprietary sprays can control them.

999 *I have seen dozens of tiny moths round my plants and there is also a black mould about. Are these connected?*

They indicate white fly attack. This can be serious. Fumigation gives control (though a double application may be needed) and some proprietary sprays kill the pest. Regular spraying also controls caterpillars which may occasionally do a lot of damage.

1000 *Spiders are making fine webs over my plants, which look dry and unhappy.*

Hot, dry conditions cause plant weakening and increase the chance of red spider attack (really it is a mite, not a spider). White oil is a traditional treatment for red spider control, and there are fumigants and aerosols you can also buy.

1001 *Is it true that there are many other possible tomato pests and diseases?*

Yes, but they rarely cause trouble to anyone who takes care to prepare the planting soil well, water regularly, feed according to a planned pattern and give good ventilation. Tomatoes are really tolerant and easy to grow. Do not worry too much about disease.